Practical Christianity

It Is For Freedom That Christ Has Set You Free

Copyright © 2012 Hilary Martinez Jr.

ISBN: 978-1-62141-880-1

All rights reserved. No part of this publication may be reproduced, stored in a retrieval system, or transmitted in any form or by any means, electronic, mechanical, recording, or otherwise, without the prior written permission of the author.

Published by BookLocker.com, Inc., Bradenton, Florida.

Printed in the United States of America on acid-free paper.

The author of this book is not a medical doctor and nothing contained in this book should be construed as medical advice. Please comply with all medical advice directed by your physician unless you and he both agree to the contrary.

Booklocker.com, Inc.
2012

First Edition

Practical Christianity

It Is For Freedom That Christ Has Set You Free

Hilary Martinez Jr.

This book is dedicated to the loving Lord who saved me, the sweet and helpful wife who stands beside me, and the wonderful children and grandchildren in whom the Lord has richly blessed me.

Contents

Introduction 1

The Big Picture 7

Groundwork 15

Sovereignty 25

Evil and its Uses 37

Suffering and its Uses 49

The Power of Submission 57

Speaking Parts 65

Swordplay 77

Unwrapping the Gifts 101

The Voice 113

Our Daily Bread 125

Self Inflicted Wounds 133

The Fruit of the Spirit 143

Practical Christianity

Foreword

This book has been a long time coming and represents a real labor of love for me. My life has changed dramatically since I accepted Christ in 1984 at the age of twenty five. The journey has been anything but easy. I have had much to learn and have tested the Lord's patience with my rebelliousness and propensity toward intellectual density. He has lived up to His Word however, by being kind, gracious, loving, and gentle with me. What is written here is a summary of the things that I have learned over the years by serious inquiry and a wholehearted attempt to grasp spiritual concepts that seemed so foreign when I began. Some of the concepts that I present in this book may seem foreign and undecipherable to the reader at times also. I ask that as you read this book, try to take it in small chunks, prayerfully seeking the Lord to help you understand what is being discussed, or to ask Him if I have received the conclusions I have reached from Him.

If I have learned anything over the years, it is to take the Word of God literally and seriously, while taking the words of men with a certain skepticism and reserve. I would expect no less here. For this reason, there are many block quotes in this work, all of them from the Word of God. It is the only definitive authority in any spiritual matter, and I do all I can to adhere to it as it is "rightly divided." All quotes are from the New International Version unless otherwise specified.

I am quite willing to interact with readers who are seriously seeking truth in a balanced and reasoned way, and can be reached at the following email address: hlmart@yahoo.com.

May this book be a blessing to you.

Practical Christianity

Introduction

Christianity is many things, but it is not a form of magic. It was never designed to provide a powerful and unseen force that would produce the perfect life in this world. We all dream of the perfect spouse, ultimate career with accolades and awards, the perfect children who are all accomplished and motivated to succeed in their God-given talents while demonstrating the proper respect to their elders and supervising adults, and the promise of a long, well funded, gracious retirement with all the trappings of success and accomplishment. That all sounds wonderful, does it not?

Lord knows that these things are possible, but most of our encounters with the power of Christian faith make it seem more like a force that is counter to these goals and disruptive to what we believe to be the path toward these ideals. Life seems to get more complicated and challenging. Is this why many believers settle for a more comfortable, watered-down version of faith? After all, we need stability, not more challenges to deal with, right?

These issues reach right down to the core of who we are as people. Does God not want us to be successful and well regarded? Do these things not bring glory to Him? After all, we move in mostly Christian circles. If I have a good, steady job, live in a nice house, and drive a nice car, is that not an outward expression of my life as a Christian? God is blessing me.

All that was just described may be absolutely right, or not. The point is that the Lord is more of a long term thinker - big picture. He knows whether or not the outward appearances are a true reflection of what resides within us. Sometimes the outward self can be a mask for what lurks below the surface. If the trappings of success are a cover to help convince ourselves and others that we are all right, when, in fact, we have things to uncover and address, those undesirable attributes have a nasty way of rearing their ugly head at the worst possible time.

Murphy's Law, one may ask? No, it is called truth. There is nothing hidden that will not be revealed (1 Timothy 5:24-25). For our Lord, it is more important that the cup be washed from the inside first (Matthew 23:25-

26). Then what is produced outwardly will be a true reflection of the internal soul.

Having internal issues to confront and contend with from a spiritual perspective are not signs of weakness. They are a reality of the world we were born into and currently reside. We all have our own set of weaknesses, insecurities, and selfishness to confront and lay at the foot of the Cross. The Bible tells us that God's ways are not our ways, or His thoughts our thoughts (Isaiah 55:8). In my view, adopting His ways, His thoughts, and His priorities are what takes us from the ordinary and mundane, and transforms us into more spiritually sentient beings; more capable of love, empathy, and unselfishness in a world that hungrily cries out for all three.

The question, then, is how do we get there from here? Is it something we ask for and receive as a blessing? Or is it a process that we undertake in order to arrive at a destination? The answer is yes. It is something to ask for in prayer, but the answer is so pervasive and life changing that, absent a transformational miracle, we must undergo a sanctifying process that slowly, carefully, and gently takes us from where we were to where we are going. A loving Savior knows what the most immediate needs are and how to deal with them in a way that does not entail ripping and tearing. It should more of a gentle stretching and reshaping.

This is where we come into the process. What is our part? Can we help? Again, the answer is yes. We are in the Hands of a loving Savior, but we are not robots. We are in a loving and long term relationship with the God who formed us from the dust. In a relationship, each person matters and has a part to play and a contribution to make.

In this book, my goal is to look at the role we play and the role that our Lord plays in the process that propels us toward our goals: the inward washing of our metaphorical cups, so that the outward cleanliness is a true reflection of who we are inside. Also, that the persons we are in the process of becoming will be healthy, thriving platforms for the bearing of the "fruit" that Jesus describes as an outward expression of spiritual growth and truth (Matthew 7:16).

In these things, God is glorified, and we are raised up to do "good works," growing in the knowledge of truth and the One who is truth. As a result, the world we live in gets incrementally better because there are more people in it with greater spiritual light residing within them, willing and energized to reach out to the spiritually needy in the love of Christ.

Chapter One

The Big Picture

In this way, love is made complete among us so that we will have confidence on the day of judgment, because in this world we are like him (1John 4:17).

Oh, to be like Him! How does *that* happen? Jesus is such an ideal for us and a role model of faith. Is it even realistic for us to imagine that we could be like Him in this world? The Bible has some things to say on this subject:

> For those God foreknew he also predestined to be conformed to the likeness of his Son, that he might be the firstborn among many brothers (Romans 8:29).

> And just as we have borne the likeness of the earthly man, so shall we bear the likeness of the man from heaven (1Corinthians 15:49).

> But whenever anyone turns to the Lord, the veil is taken away. And we, who with unveiled faces all reflect the Lord's glory, are being transformed into his likeness with ever-increasing glory,

which comes from the Lord, who is the Spirit (2Corinthians 3:16, 18).

The idea seems overwhelming because the distance between who Jesus is and the people we know ourselves to be is so great. It is a work, however, that God does out of His amazing love for us. It really is a labor of love in which our Father in heaven has a tremendous investment; the blood of His holy, innocent Son.

Jesus' blood has power in it to not only redeem us from the curse of the Law and wash away our sin; it also has the power to help us overcome the "world." Why is this so crucial? I am not sure if you have noticed, but there seems to a malevolent force (the Bible calls it evil) in our world that wants to oppose that which is godly and brings truth and light into our individual lives and therefore the circles in which we reside. That opposition is a small clue as to the eternal power and value of the truth that resides in the Word of God and the expression of that truth in us as we walk through our lives and endeavor to embody the reality of God's grace.

Overcoming that darkness seems to be a vital step in our own development as believers and followers of Christ.

Is it possible to overcome in this way? The Bible tells us that it is, ("They overcame him by the blood of the Lamb and by the word of their testimony; they did not love their lives so much as to shrink from death." [Revelation 12:11]), but it will not happen without help. Our personal relationship to the Lord is vital for this task. He is the only One who can guide us in the "paths of righteousness" (Psalms 23:3) that make it possible. This is the "narrow road" (Matthew 7:14), and it is a challenging and stretching journey into the heart of God and the love of Christ. I can tell you from my own experience that nothing else makes life so worth every minute. It is filled with awe and wonder as the God of the universe makes Himself known and demonstrates His power and glory in the face of all opposition and hindrance.

Does this sound like something one could and should undertake considering the magnitude of the obstacles? If it were not, the rewards for going through this test would not be so great. Listen to the promises that are reserved for those who make it through to the other side:

To him who overcomes, I will give the right to eat from the tree of life, which is in the paradise of God (Revelation 2:7b).

He who overcomes will not be hurt at all by the second death (Revelation 2:11b).

To him who overcomes, I will give some of the hidden manna. I will also give him a white stone with a new name written on it, known only to him who receives it (Revelation 2:17b).

To him who overcomes and does my will to the end, I will give authority over the nations--'He will rule them with an iron scepter; he will dash them to pieces like pottery' --just as I have received authority from my Father. I will also give him the morning star (Revelation 2:26-28).

He who overcomes will, like them, be dressed in white. I will never blot out his name from the book of life, but will acknowledge his name before my Father and his angels (Revelation 3:5).

Him who overcomes I will make a pillar in the temple of my God. Never again will he leave it. I will write on him the name of my God and the name of the city of my God, the new Jerusalem, which is coming down out of heaven from my God; and I will also write on him my new name (Revelation 3:12).

> To him who overcomes, I will give the right to sit with me on my throne, just as I overcame and sat down with my Father on his throne (Revelation 3:21).
>
> He who overcomes will inherit all this, and I will be his God and he will be my son (Revelation 21:7).

This, friends, is a "wow!" It is impossible to overstate the seriousness and amazing magnitude of these promises. We cannot fathom what it all means, but it is surely safe to say that these are the most worthwhile of goals since the Word assures us that it is doable and eminently possible by God's grace. Stepping onto this path is something that takes courage and trust that God is able to keep us from harm and deliver us safely to the other side. It is my contention that in going through this process, the believer is transformed because they are subjected to a new way of thinking and reacting to various circumstances.

We are all, to one degree or another, products of our environments. We learn from the world around us how to deal with the things that we confront in our lives. It is modeled for us by our parents, our siblings, our peers, television and movies, and from an ever broadening array of media sources, including news media pundits, who let us know whether or not some situation should outrage us.

In most cases, and from a worldly perspective, we are programmed or conditioned to respond to unexpected circumstances with either anger or fear. Even in Christian homes, faith responses are seemingly rare and infrequent. This is an indication that a "renewing of the mind" (Romans 12:2) is necessary, and we are all at different stages of this most crucial transformation process.

Interestingly enough, the "world" around us seems to be most perceptive when we do not respond in an expected way and moves in quickly to try and quell what it sees as rebellion against it and its way of doing business. "They think it strange that you do not plunge with them into the same flood of dissipation, and they heap abuse on you" (1Peter 4:4). This, of course, is a form of rejection, and normally, we do not handle rejection very well. "Blessed are you when men hate you, when they exclude you and insult you and reject your name as evil, because of the Son of Man. Rejoice in that day and leap for joy, because great is your reward in heaven. For that is how their fathers treated the prophets" (Luke 6:22-23). For the short term, and until the "end of the age," this is why fellowship with the Triune God and other believers is so important. We are buoyed by the strength and success of those further down the path. "He who walks with the wise grows wise, but a companion of fools suffers harm" (Proverbs 13:20).

So, what are we giving up and what are we receiving in return? We are giving up our old lives that we have made a muddle of, in most cases (especially mine), and trading it for a new life in Christ that is filled with the love of God and the fellowship of the Savior and the Holy Spirit for an eternity. We are also walking away from a world system that is crashing right before our eyes and embracing the Kingdom of God and His way of doing things that last forever. We are walking away from a fleeting vapor of a lifespan that rapidly degrades on the downhill side and embracing an eternal life that never fades or diminishes over the span of eternity. That is a trade I am very willing to make.

> But you have come to Mount Zion, to the
> heavenly Jerusalem, the city of the living God.
> You have come to thousands upon thousands of
> angels in joyful assembly, to the church of the
> firstborn, whose names are written in heaven.

Hilary Martinez Jr.

You have come to God, the judge of all men, to the spirits of righteous men made perfect, to Jesus the mediator of a new covenant, and to the sprinkled blood that speaks a better word than the blood of Abel (Hebrews 12:22-24).

Welcome!

Chapter Two

Groundwork

By the grace God has given me, I laid a foundation as an expert builder, and someone else is building on it. But each one should be careful how he builds. For no one can lay any foundation other than the one already laid, which is Jesus Christ.
(1Corinthians 3:10-11)

For the purposes of this book, it is assumed that the reader is a believer and has asked the Lord into his or her heart. If this is not the case, I invite you to receive the Lord Jesus as your Savior. It will be the start of a journey of discovery like none other in this world. The truth is a powerful elixir, and the benefits of embracing that truth are absolutely life changing and exciting in a way that nothing else could ever match. It is truly an adventurous odyssey with the power of heaven to watch over you and guide you around and through the challenges. Are the stakes high? How about life and death! Yes, it is quite serious, but just getting out of bed in the morning can be a perilous struggle. What about driving a car, or flying in an airplane? Life is all about managed risk and the benefits of taking on that risk. One can never find a more profound safe harbor than being firmly ensconced in the will of God for one's life, and no greater benefit than the relationship with Jesus Christ, with eternal life to cap it all off.

Then, no matter what goes on, and death is reasonably certain at some point, you will have at least lived life to the fullest while you were here. One does not want to die having never truly lived. "In him was life, and that life was the light of men" (John 1:4). If you call on His Name and ask Him to save you from the penalty of sin and reveal Himself to you, He will do so. He died and was raised again that you might at least have that opportunity. This is between you and the Savior. Please do not allow the influence of other people's opinions to keep you from the most wonderful life possible.

My very first client as a Christian counselor was a man in his mid to late thirties who came in because of anger issues. Anger had been a problem in his marriage and it had been the issue that led to their divorce. He was now living in a different state than his wife and two boys, but anger was now becoming an issue between him and the young lady he was seeing and spending time with.

He related to me how he had grown up in a home where his Mom had taken him and his brother to church regularly, and he and his wife had been very active in their church for a number of years, helping with children's ministry and generally participating in many aspects of the church ministry. They began to quarrel about financial issues after some setbacks, and things began to unravel. As I was attempting to establish a spiritual history of the client, I asked him about his conversion experience; the time when he had accepted Christ as Lord. He became lost in thought for a few moments, and then told me that he could not really remember having done so. He had been deeply involved in church, but had never given his heart to the Lord! Needless to say, we prayed the sinner's prayer in my office that day and we had a joyous time of rejoicing over God's grace. That was the last time I saw that client. He had found his answer. I still pray for him when I think about him.

We cannot assume anything in this journey. Each one of us needs to have that personal experience of conversion.

We are certainly not saved because of church attendance. As a practical matter, please examine your own experience and know that you have made that step of faith by asking the Lord into your heart to redeem you from the curse and cover your sin. There is an exchange that happens behind the scenes when we seek and find God's grace in Christ. God delivers us from the "dominion of darkness" and brings us into the "kingdom of the Son He loves." (Colossians 1:13). This experience, whether we feel it with our five senses or not, is the game changer that makes everything else promised in the Bible possible and applicable to us as individuals.

Now, there is another step here that should be addressed, and that is the concept of baptism. In the Book of Acts, the Apostle Peter gave a sermon that stirred the hearts of those listening. They asked, "What shall we do?" Peter replied, "Repent and be baptized, every one of you, in the name of Jesus Christ for the forgiveness of your sins. And you will receive the gift of the Holy Spirit" (Acts 2:38). When we sprinkle infants for the remission of sin, in case of a premature death, they do not repent of their sin. They have no conception of sin. I am in no way suggesting that infants who die tragically are in danger of hell based on a lack of repentance. I am of the opinion that they are not held accountable until they learn right from wrong. God is just. Even our Lord had to learn how to differentiate right from wrong, but it was not sin before he understood.

> Therefore the Lord Himself will give you a sign: Behold, a virgin will be with child and bear a son, and she will call His name Immanuel. He will eat curds and honey at the time He knows enough to refuse evil and choose good (Isaiah 7:14-15, NASB).

I am also not against the practice of sprinkling infants. It provides great comfort to parents and grandparents to believe that their little ones have been covered by God's grace should something unforeseen occur.

My focus is on baptism as a portal and necessary component of "entering the Kingdom of God." I am not convinced that infant sprinkling accomplishes this most important component of life in the Spirit. Jesus said, "I tell you the truth, no one can see the kingdom of God unless he is born again" (John 3:3), and that, "I tell you the truth, no one can enter the kingdom of God unless he is born of water and the Spirit" (John 3:5). Infants are baptized because they were born. Is it possible that they might need to be baptized a second time later on to be "born again?" "Flesh gives birth to flesh, but the Spirit gives birth to spirit" (John 3:6).

> Or don't you know that all of us who were baptized into Christ Jesus were baptized into his death? *We were therefore buried with him through baptism into death* in order that, just as Christ was raised from the dead through the glory of the Father, *we too may live a new life.* If we have been united with him like this in his death, we will certainly also be united with him in his resurrection. For we know that our old self was crucified with him so that the body of sin might be done away with, that we should no longer be slaves to sin--because anyone who has died has been freed from sin. Now if we died with Christ, we believe that we will also live with him. For we know that since Christ was raised from the dead, he cannot die again; death no longer has mastery over him. The death he died, he died to sin once for all; but the life he lives, he lives to God. In the same way, count yourselves dead to sin but alive to God in Christ Jesus (Romans 6:3-11, emphasis mine).

Baptism described in this passage of Romans is quite a bit different than the purpose of infant baptism. Again, I am not demeaning infant baptism, I only want to point out the different purposes for each. Many of my Catholic friends feel that their faith in the Lord and infant baptism is all they need to live the Christian life. I have no doubt of their salvation; my concern is for the "new life" this passage refers to. We all need to enter into the Kingdom in order to be on the same spiritual plane and embrace the spiritual concepts taught in the Word and promoted by the Spirit. "The man without the Spirit does not accept the things that come from the Spirit of God, for they are foolishness to him, and he cannot understand them, because they are spiritually discerned" (1Corinthians 2:14).

If you are a denominational leader in a denomination that only does infant baptism, will you please consider this subject and possibly try an experimental baptism on a small test group of those above the age of accountability (6 years or higher, depending on the person) to see if there is any difference? What might the difference be if there was a spiritual change from before to after? I would expect the reading and understanding of Scripture to be much more meaningful and of more depth. I would also expect a deeper and more profound discernment of the Lord in the heart of the believer within a day or so. When I was baptized, my heart came alive with the love of Christ and the gift of "living waters" (John 7:38).

If you are a member of a denomination that only does infant baptism, would you consider being baptized into the death of Christ as the Bible describes? As an adult, you can both repent and be baptized, being born then of water and Spirit. One does not have to be baptized within the walls of a church. It can be done in a pool, hot tub, lake, pond, river, or any other body of water where you can be fully submerged. Everything must be "buried" under the water. We would not want any surviving "flesh" that was not identified with the death of the Lord. We want to be "all in," as they say.

The point here is not to undermine any denominational heritage, but to use care in "how we build" on the foundation of Christ (1Corinthians 3:10b). When we stand before the Lord, our denominations will not be there to defend us. It will be us and the Lord, and we want to get it right. There is no risk in being baptized in the Spirit, but potentially great spiritual gain.

Please seek the Lord about this issue and ask Him to reveal to you whether or not you are being led by the Spirit, for "those who are led by the Spirit of God are sons of God" (Romans 8:14).

Chapter Three

Sovereignty

All the peoples of the earth are regarded as nothing. He does as he pleases with the powers of heaven and the peoples of the earth. No one can hold back his hand or say to him: "What have you done?" (Daniel 4:35)

Is the world we live in random and chaotic or ordered and orchestrated? If you are like most people, this concept of God's sovereignty will really stretch your understanding of Biblical truth. It is, however, crucially important. We must wrap our understanding around this reality to be able to really rest in God's goodness for us. One of my top five favorite verses in Scripture is Jeremiah 29:11: "For I know the plans I have for you," declares the LORD, "plans to prosper you and not to harm you, plans to give you hope and a future." In order to make His plans prevail over my circumstances, the Lord would have to be in charge of quite a bit of life. But I do not reside in a bubble. There are interactions we make every day that seem to have some bearing on our circumstances and available opportunities.

The Scriptures on this subject are quite striking. "In his heart a man plans his course, but the LORD determines his steps" (Proverbs 16:9). "Many are the plans in a man's heart, but it is the LORD's purpose that prevails" (Proverbs 19:21). All right, He must be referring to the lives of believers. "The LORD works out everything for his own ends--even the wicked for a day of disaster" (Proverbs 16:4). This is getting deeper – "even the wicked." This is a lot to think about.

These are interesting proverbs, but the Bible must have more to say about this. We all have to make choices in our lives. Those choices determine the life we lead and the direction we take. Is the Lord telling us that He is behind those choices we make? "I know, O LORD, that a man's life is not his own; it is not for man to direct his steps" (Jeremiah 10:23). This is a remarkable statement - but what about the choices we face every day? We have to make our *own* choices!

> This day I call heaven and earth as witnesses against you that I have set before you life and death, blessings and curses. Now choose life, so that you and your children may live...
> (Deuteronomy 30:19).

There, you see, the people are asked to make a choice for themselves. Also, in the Book of Joshua:

> But if serving the LORD seems undesirable to you, then choose for yourselves this day whom you will serve, whether the gods your forefathers served beyond the River, or the gods of the Amorites, in whose land you are living. But as for me and my household, we will serve the LORD (Joshua 24:15).

Whew! That is kind of a relief, is it not? We would like to have *some* say in the matter. Making good decisions makes us feel good about ourselves.

What about the idea of God's purposes? How does that fit in with the choices that we have to make? What does the New Testament say about this subject? We are asked to make a decision for Christ, are we not? Our eternity depends on it.

Actually, John 15:16 tells us: "You did not choose me, but I chose you and appointed you to go and bear fruit-- fruit that will last. Then the Father will give you whatever you ask in my name." This is what is commonly called "flipping the script." He chose us? Wow! We must have done something in the enterprise. "No one can come to me unless the Father who sent me draws him, and I will raise him up at the last day" (John 6:44). This is sounding like an exclusive club with limited entry. Entering into a relationship with the Lord Jesus is truly a miraculous privilege. Maybe we did not realize just *how* miraculous. Faith in Christ is open to all, but remember: "For many are invited, but few are chosen" (Matthew 22:14). It sounds like we should not be asking people to make a decision for Christ, but asking Jesus to make a decision for *them*.

How, then, do we square the issue of decision making with the Scripture? Somehow we must discern or discover God's will for ourselves so that we can answer His call and honor Him with our lives. Consider Philippians 2:12b-13: "...continue to work out your salvation with fear and trembling, *for it is God who works in you to will and to act according to his good purpose*" (emphasis mine). Please take a moment and try to get your mind around this statement. Can you hear the echo of Jeremiah 29:11 here? "I know the plans I have for you, says the Lord..."...God who works in you to will and to act according to *his good purpose*. How about the Proverbs and "it is the Lord's purpose that prevails" (19:21). This sounds like something that may take some time to grasp. I thought we were not robots? For one thing, we must get our understanding around something the Apostle Paul told us in 1Corinthians 6:19-20a: "Do you not know that your body is a temple of the Holy Spirit, who is in you, whom you have received from God? *You are not your own; you were bought at a price"* (emphasis mine).

Lord means master or owner. If Jesus is our Lord, we are not our own. Is that all right with you? Was that a fair trade? Should submission to God's will for me be a cause for concern? No. His purposes for me are good. His plans are to prosper me and to give me a hope and future! I can rest in Him and trust Him that He has good planned for me, not evil (Romans 8:28).

All that may be true, but I am still not a zombie. Where do I fit in to all this? Jonathan Edwards (1703-1799), a prominent New England preacher who was an instrumental figure in one of America's most profound revivals, and widely regarded as an astonishing philosophical theologian, contended that as long as men are free to do as they will, they are a free moral agent. Freedom comes, then, from being able to do as one wills.

What God reveals in Philippians is that He is working upstream of our will, ensuring that His purposes are carried out. For me, this is extremely satisfying. God's will is done. I do as I will, trusting God that what I manage to accomplish was His good purpose in me.

Now, back to the question of overall sovereignty, Matthew 10:29 states:

> Are not two sparrows sold for a penny? *Yet not one of them will fall to the ground apart from the will of your Father.* And even the very hairs of your head are all numbered. So don't be afraid; you are worth more than many sparrows (emphasis mine).

This is another stunning statement of God's sovereignty. Is this a good reason not to be fearful? It certainly works for me! It is hard to get one's mind around such broad, sweeping statements, but if I truly accept what is being conveyed here, I can walk down the street with no worries. Am I saying that nothing bad can happen? Only if God wills it, and I am resting on His promises like, "I have given you authority to trample on snakes and scorpions and to overcome all the power of the enemy; *nothing will harm you* (Luke 10:19, emphasis mine). Also, Psalm 91:

He will cover you with his feathers, and under his wings you will find refuge; his faithfulness will be your shield and rampart. You will not fear the terror of night, nor the arrow that flies by day, nor the pestilence that stalks in the darkness, nor the plague that destroys at midday. A thousand may fall at your side, ten thousand at your right hand, but it will not come near you. You will only observe with your eyes and see the punishment of the wicked. If you make the Most High your dwelling--even the LORD, who is my refuge--then no harm will befall you, no disaster will come near your tent. For he will command his angels concerning you to guard you in all your ways; they will lift you up in their hands, so that you will not strike your foot against a stone. You will tread upon the lion and the cobra; you will trample the great lion and the serpent. "Because he loves me," says the LORD, "I will rescue him; I will protect him, for he acknowledges my name. He will call upon me, and I will answer him; I will be with him in trouble, I will deliver him and honor him. With long life will I satisfy him and show him my salvation." (Verses 4-16)

It is so comforting to know that our awesome God is capable of protecting us from what seems crazy and chaotic around us.

There is another passage that I would like to present to you because in my mind it is the definitive Scripture on this subject. It is in Romans chapter nine and concerns the twins Jacob and Esau.

> Not only that, but Rebekah's children had one and the same father, our father Isaac. Yet, *before the twins were born or had done anything good or bad*--in order that God's purpose in election might stand: not by works but by him who calls--she was told, "The older will serve the younger." Just as it is written: "Jacob I loved, but Esau I hated." What then shall we say? *Is God unjust?* Not at all! For he says to Moses, "I will have mercy on whom I have mercy, and I will have compassion on whom I have compassion." *It does not, therefore, depend on man's desire or effort, but on God's mercy.* For the Scripture says to Pharaoh: "I raised you up for this very purpose, that I might display my power in you and that my name might be proclaimed in all the earth." *Therefore God has mercy on whom he wants to have mercy, and he hardens whom he wants to harden.* One of you will say to me: "Then why does God still blame us? *For who resists his will?"* But who are you, O man, to talk back to God? "Shall what is formed say to him who formed it, 'Why did you make me like this?'" Does not the potter have the right to make out of the same lump of clay some pottery for noble

purposes and some for common use? What if God, choosing to show his wrath and make his power known, bore with great patience the objects of his wrath--prepared for destruction? What if he did this to make the riches of his glory known to the objects of his mercy, whom he prepared in advance for glory--even us, whom he also called, not only from the Jews but also from the Gentiles? (Romans 9:10-24, emphasis mine)

Honestly, I do not even know what to say about this passage. It is such a bold declaration of a sovereign God that my words in commentary seem absolutely meaningless and trivial. To me, it is saying that God is absolutely in command of history and the lives of individual people, and that we are helpless to do anything but rest in His goodness and mercy toward us. It humbles me and makes me grateful for His mercy toward *me*. When I first read this, I was absolutely stunned and in despair for those outside of the mercy of Christ, especially my family members who are not believers. What if they were being hardened and had no chance of salvation? I was in distress for a day or so before God relieved me with an amazing scripture that I would like to share here. It is another passage in Romans: "For God has bound all men over to disobedience so that he may have mercy on them all" (11:32). This is another broad sweeping statement that just floored me, but it really gave me a profound sense of hope for the lost.

I realize that this sounds a lot like universal salvation, and I do not subscribe to that idea. There will be a separation of sheep and goats at the final judgment (Matthew 25:32). The world obviously contains some of each.

Having said that however, we must remember that the Lord has promised to pour out His Spirit on all flesh (Joel 2:28). Also, the Lord made this amazing statement through the prophet Jeremiah: "No longer will a man teach his neighbor, or a man his brother, saying, 'Know the LORD,' because they will all know me, from the least of them to the greatest" (Jeremiah 31:34).

These issues are difficult to sort out because they *seem* contradictory, but I have full confidence that God's plan will prevail and it gives me hope that there is at least a chance for lost souls to be saved.

Practical Christianity

Our God truly is an awesome God. He reigns from heaven above, with wisdom, power, and love. Our God is an awesome God.

Chapter Four

Evil and its Uses

Evil will slay the wicked; the foes of the righteous will be condemned.

(Psalms 34:21)

There are a number of questions that confront Christians in our modern world. In the movies, there is always a set of villains in any adventure story or tale of discovery. The Indiana Jones movies come to mind. There has to be a tension between the main characters of the story and a nefarious group who is competing with them and attempting to keep them from reaching their noble goals for the sordid ends of the antagonists. Is this art imitating life?

I think we can all agree that evil exists in our world. It manifests itself in the hearts of men and rears its ugly head in a variety of ways: anger, greed, thirst for power, murder, adulterous affairs, corruption, lies; and these are just the politicians! All right, sorry! That was a cheap shot.

Look, we joke about it because it is so serious. We all wish it were less real and pervasive in our surroundings. We even have to watch for it in our own hearts and lives. Nobody is exempt from temptation; and temptation is the sales pitch of evil. Evil wants to have its way with us and ruin us and our testimony of God's grace and goodness. Somehow, we need to reconcile the reality that God is good and lives in us as believers, yet there remains this constant tension that is trying to disrupt the flow of blessings and goodness we all crave from God. In the Book of Genesis, God gives Cain some excellent counsel: "If you do what is right, will you not be accepted? But if you do not do what is right, sin is crouching at your door; it desires to have you, but you must master it" (Genesis 4:7).

Are sin and evil the same thing? That is one great theological question. In my view, and for the purposes of this discussion, sin is the fleshly desire that once was in control of the person without Christ. The flesh can succumb to the temptation of evil, causing one to sin, and as a consequence produce a form of bondage in the heart and spirit of the believer unless there is genuine repentance, the grace of God, and the blood of Christ to neutralize it.

What about evil, then? What is its purpose and why does it exist? This question began for me after reading the book of Job. The book of Job has been an eye opener and the source of many theological questions over the centuries. Mine centered on the collegial conversation that God had with the devil. To me, it was like our president having lunch with Bin Laden, the vilest of villains. How was this possible? I was thinking, "Lord, instead of talking to him like an old friend, why did you not reach over there and choke the life out of him?" I was really upset about it. Imagine the suffering in this world that would have been alleviated had that occurred. Obviously, there was more to this than I was able to grasp at that time, so I asked the Lord to give me wisdom.

One of the things that I had heard as a young believer was that God and the devil were equal and opposite forces for light and darkness in a constant titanic battle for the hearts and souls of men. As men lived their lives, this battle went on until one side or the other had its way in each person's existence. This turned out to be completely false. God is God. The devil is a tool. This is the Scripture God showed me that changed my perception completely and instantly:

> I am the LORD, and there is no other; apart
> from me there is no God. I will strengthen you,
> though you have not acknowledged me, so that
> from the rising of the sun to the place of its
> setting men may know there is none besides me.
> I am the LORD, and there is no other. *I form the
> light and create darkness, I bring prosperity
> and create disaster; I, the LORD, do all these
> things* (Isaiah 45:5-7, emphasis mine).

This information is faith stretching, but makes abundantly clear that God is in charge. One God – forms light and creates darkness – brings prosperity and creates disaster – does all these things. My perception of who God is changed forever with this revelation. It takes time for this to sink in. How do I reconcile this with a God that is all good? What it meant was that some things that I perceived as evil may actually be something else - justice? wrath? consequences of sin?

King Nebuchadnezzar in the book of Daniel had learned some hard lessons about God. This was one of his conclusions after going through some amazing trials:

> "Now I, Nebuchadnezzar, praise and exalt and
> glorify the King of heaven, because everything he
> does is right and all his ways are just. And those
> who walk in pride he is able to humble." (Daniel
> 4:37)

Everything He does is right and all His ways are just. If God makes it happen, it is right and just. We have already established God's sovereignty, so there is no doubt that all things do work together for good (Romans 8:28).

Everyone asks about violent storms and natural catastrophe. How does a good God allow such things? Are not innocent people killed? Good question. The Scripture is clear that:

> The LORD is slow to anger and great in power; the LORD will not leave the guilty unpunished. His way is in the whirlwind and the storm, and clouds are the dust of his feet. (Nahum 1:3)

> Disaster will come upon you, and you will not know how to conjure it away. A calamity will fall upon you that you cannot ward off with a ransom; a catastrophe you cannot foresee will suddenly come upon you. (Isaiah 47:11)

> Yet how often is the lamp of the wicked snuffed out? How often does calamity come upon them, the fate God allots in his anger? (Job 21:17)

> When a trumpet sounds in a city, do not the people tremble? When disaster comes to a city, has not the LORD caused it? (Amos 3:6)

Ever notice that after there has been a terrible disaster and they are doing a flyover of the area to show the devastation, there are always one or two houses that were somehow completely untouched by the destructive power of the storm? God knows how to protect those who are calling upon His name and standing on His Word. Does this mean that godly people or innocent children cannot die in such calamities? No, but this world is not where final justice occurs. All of our lives on this planet have a definitive span that is determined by God's grace (Hebrews 9:27).

Now, back to the concept of evil: God is not evil - what He does is not evil. God is just and His judgments are right. Evil, then, is the enforcement arm of the curse that mankind was placed under after Adam sinned (Romans 8:20). The verdict was pronounced in God's judgment over Adam and therefore mankind in the future (Genesis 3:14-19). The consequences of disobedience and the ensuing bondage ensures that God's Word came to pass concerning the consequences of partaking of the "forbidden fruit" (Genesis 2:17).

Evil, embodied by the devil, and administered by evil spirits, was given authority over all men born under the curse (Luke 4:6). For those who have not accepted Christ, the case was closed at the time of Adam. They are mastered by evil and have no say in the matter (1John 5:19). The world had become like a penal colony with a very cruel master to oversee it.

Enter the Savior; Jesus Christ is born of a virgin and came to earth with a very special mission. The toll of the suffering on earth had reached into a Father's heart and stirred His compassion (John 3:16). He would provide a source of salvation and a means to escape the bondage of the curse. Praise be to our Lord! "...because through Christ Jesus the law of the Spirit of life set me free from the law of sin and death" (Romans 8:2). Without Christ, we remain under God's wrath: "Whoever believes in the Son has eternal life, but whoever rejects the Son will not see life, for God's wrath remains on him" (John 3:36).

So, for believers, they have been wrested from the "dominion of darkness" and have been brought "into the kingdom of the Son he loves" (Colossians 1:3). Does that mean that the battle is over? Mission accomplished? Well, yes, except for one little thing: the issue of sin and the flesh. Let us call it some unfinished business. Temptation still exists. Sin certainly can rear its ugly head. Now, there *is* some courtroom drama. *This* case remains open until the final trumpet. Imagine an invisible courtroom with a judge: God (James 4:12), an advocate or defense attorney: Jesus (Hebrews 7:25), and a prosecutor (the devil is called the "accuser of the brothers, who accuses them before our God day and night" (Revelation 12:10).

The charges are not formal; we do not face our accuser, and innocence or guilt is determined by the facts and not fancy arguments. Even though the devil spends day and night accusing the saints of wrongdoing, thankfully the Judge is righteous and the evidence is clear. We are either guilty of the charges or we are not. If we are guilty, there is a price to pay and we have opened the door to evil and given it a foothold (Ephesians 4:27) in our life. "Like a fluttering sparrow or a darting swallow, an undeserved curse does not come to rest. A whip for the horse, a halter for the donkey, and a rod for the backs of fools!" (Proverbs 26:2-3). If we deserve it because we have been found guilty, look out, the door to spiritual attack has been opened. Confession, repentance, and grace are necessary. Absent these things, we can walk around for a long time wondering where we left the path. You are not notified by a process server or certified mail, it just happens. We call it evil. Is it? One thing we know for sure; suffering occurs when we are found guilty.

As a matter of practicality, friends, do all you can to be free of any form of guilt. Do not lie, steal, or cheat. Whatever you gain will not be worth it.

> Why should any living man complain when punished for his sins? (Lamentations 3:39)

> You only have I chosen of all the families of the earth; therefore I will punish you for all your sins. (Amos 3:2)

> We are punished justly, for we are getting what our deeds deserve. But this man [Jesus] has done nothing wrong. (Luke 23:41)

> Anyone who does wrong will be repaid for his wrong, and there is no favoritism. (Colossians 3:25)

> ...and that in this matter no one should wrong his brother or take advantage of him. The Lord will punish men for all such sins, as we have already told you and warned you. (1Thessalonians 4:6)

> So I will cast her on a bed of suffering, and I will make those who commit adultery with her suffer intensely, unless they repent of her ways. (Revelation 2:22)

There is a pervasive and persistent pattern here of the cause and effect relationship between wrongdoing and the suffering that is resulting from God administering justice. This type of suffering is something we should cry out to God to help us avoid. It is well worth the effort.

Now, why is it so important for us to know that God does punish disobedience and irreverence? In our modern society, the tendency has been for people to fear the devil instead of fearing God. The reverence that belongs to our awesome God goes the wrong way. We cannot let the devil have any of God's glory! That is absolutely unacceptable. Are we trying to preserve God's reputation? That would be a devastating mistake.

> The fear of the LORD is the beginning of knowledge, but fools despise wisdom and discipline (Proverbs 1:7).

> The fear of the LORD is the beginning of wisdom, and knowledge of the Holy One is understanding (Proverbs 9:10).

The fear of the Lord is the beginning of knowledge and wisdom, and knowing God *is* understanding. Are we lacking any of that in our modern society? I pray that the

Body of Christ understands the crucial nature of this subject.

What about God being love? How do we reconcile this fear inspiring God with the God of love? Parents who discipline their children *are* doing it out of love, even if the child does not think so. It *is* right, and it is in the best interests of the child. Parents who demand that their children show them proper respect *are* loving their child. Respect for authority will serve them well when they are older and they will respect you for demanding what you, as a parent, are rightfully due. Good parents know when loving kindness, gentleness, and playfulness are appropriate, and when to put a halt to behavior or attitudes that are unacceptable.

It is no different with our awesome Creator. Not only is He more than due our reverence, but it is in *our* best interest that He makes sure we understand that concept. He is not to be trifled with and it would behoove us all to understand that before we appear before Him. The idea that God is just this lovey, squishy plaything that we take or leave at our leisure is just a fantasy. Taking Him too lightly has hurt every one of us. It allows evil to be elevated far above its station. God will not punish evil if we fear it instead of Him. It is no wonder that Christianity has become a mockery.

I heard a story about Europe's primary education system. One of our American educators was surprised that they taught religion to all their students. Can you imagine that in America? They explained that religion was an important and deeply ingrained part of their cultural history. "Besides," they said, "who is afraid of a toothless lion?"

Chapter 5

Suffering and its Uses

For it has been granted to you on behalf of Christ not only to believe on him, but also to suffer for him... (Philippians 1:29)

Suffering -- right. Now, there is a subject that brings people running. Is it safe to say that the rose has a thorn? Putting a happy face on the subject of suffering is quite a challenge. The first thing we need to know about suffering is that it is a double edged sword, so to speak. One can suffer for doing wrong, as we have seen in the previous chapter; or suffering can be done for the sake of the Lord and the Gospel of Christ.

> But how is it to your credit if you receive a beating for doing wrong and endure it? But if you suffer for doing good and you endure it, this is commendable before God. To this you were called, because Christ suffered for you, leaving you an example, that you should follow in his steps. (1Peter 2:20-21)

I applied for a number of jobs as a Spiritual Formation Pastor or Discipleship Pastor at large churches. The main question they had was, "Why is the Body of Christ not growing and maturing?" My view is that it centers on this issue of suffering. If anything we do or say draws any kind of spiritual pushback, we back away. Let us face the facts; suffering is not fun. Suffering makes it hard to keep my mask of "all rightness" on.

Suffering, however, has a specific, targeted purpose that is designed to be limited by the Lord's grace. As in the book of Job, there will be specific parameters established in every situation, and the duration of the circumstances is something we can have a say in. The quicker we learn what the suffering is intended to teach us, the sooner it ends and we can move on. "See, I have refined you, though not as silver; I have tested you in the furnace of affliction" (Isaiah 48:10). The key here is to know that what we suffer is not for doing wrong, but for doing what is right. How do we know the difference? Great question, and this will lead us right into some very practical Christianity.

When some type of storm arises in your life, one can ask the Lord to reveal to your heart if the circumstances you are facing are because of something that you have said or done. Then, go into your room and close the door. "But when you pray, go into your room, close the door, and pray to your Father, who is unseen. Then your Father, who sees what is done in secret, will reward you" (Matthew 6:6). I usually kneel down next to the bed and do my best to "still" myself. "The LORD will fight for you; you need only to be still" (Exodus 14:14). In my view, this means quieting my thoughts. It is one of the most challenging things I have ever tried to do. "This is what the Sovereign LORD, the Holy One of Israel, says: 'In repentance and rest is your salvation, in quietness and trust is your strength...'" (Isaiah 30: 15). "Be still before the LORD and wait patiently for him; do not fret when men succeed in their ways, when they carry out their wicked schemes" (Psalms 37:7).

Now we are into the meat and potatoes. This will be a revelation to some, but there are people out there who delight in wickedness and love to devise schemes against the righteous. Shocking, right? I know, but it is true. The bottom line is that there are a multitude of people in our world who love darkness and are doing their best to comfortably reside in what is fast becoming "gross darkness" (Isaiah 60:2, KJV). "This is the verdict: Light has come into the world, but men loved darkness instead of light because their deeds were evil" (John 3:19). Now, here comes "ol' megawatt" sporting the light of Christ and shining it around like a five million candle power spotlight right into their comfort zone. They will do anything they can to stomp out that light. It is painful to them.

One thing we need to understand is that the lost and hurting are out there in that darkness. If we can bear up under the onslaught of opposition, by the grace of God and the love of Christ, the light will draw those people in and they can be ministered to in the Lord's love for them.

When we realize that Jesus left His comfort zone to come to the earth and die for us, it makes it easier for us to go through whatever it takes to reach those for whom the Lord's compassion burns. We have been given a tremendous opportunity to be the arms and hands of Christ extended to the poor. "See, darkness covers the earth and thick darkness is over the peoples, but the LORD rises upon you and his glory appears over you" (Isaiah 60:2). As we seek the Lord and learn to trust in Him, His glory will manifest in us. It is a challenge, but well worth the effort. The personal benefits and the resulting ministry that stems from our willingness to share in the Lord's work will last forever.

How about those personal benefits; can suffering actually be good for me? "Although he was a son, he learned obedience from what he suffered" (Hebrews 5:8). "Therefore, since Christ suffered in his body, arm yourselves also with the same attitude, because he who has suffered in his body is done with sin" (1Peter 4:1). Done with sin - that is an interesting statement. Does this imply that if one refuses to submit to suffering, they do not feel as if they are done with sin? Are they trying to straddle the fence, in case there is something over there they may be interested in? Could this be a form of "double mindedness" (James 1:8)? I do not want to be accusatory, but posing the question may be thought provoking.

When we understand what suffering actually means, we will see it as a privilege. I know that sounds kind of "out there," but suffering broadens our perspective. It helps us to draw near to the Lord. He loves us through our trials, knowing that we do it out of love and devotion to Him.

> Not only so, but we also rejoice in our sufferings, because we know that suffering produces perseverance; perseverance, character; and character, hope. And hope does not disappoint us, because God has poured out his love into our hearts by the Holy Spirit, whom he has given us (Romans 5:3-5).

It is a great way of saying "thank you" for loving me when I was lost in sin and pulling me out, granting me an eternal hope. It recognizes that there are many people out there as lost as I was that need the Lord's love.

Who was willing to suffer so that I might be saved? In my own life, I am reminded of a man I worked with who came to Christ. He told all of us about his conversion and the love of God in Christ. We all listened politely, but what we heard made no sense to us, so we did what everyone probably does in a case like this; we made fun of him and his salvation behind his back. At one point, my car was having an issue and I caught a ride to work with Bill and his girlfriend. They played Christian music both there and back. I remember telling my then girlfriend that it was like riding in a "rolling cathedral." Even though we made sport of him, what he said had an impact on us. There are more than a few in the group who have since become believers.

He probably does not even know what his testimony accomplished. His suffering was not all that bad, but the consequences will last throughout eternity.

> Therefore we do not lose heart. Though outwardly we are wasting away, yet inwardly we are being renewed day by day. For our light and momentary troubles are achieving for us an eternal glory that far outweighs them all. So we fix our eyes not on what is seen, but on what is unseen. For what is seen is temporary, but what is unseen is eternal (2Corinthians 4:16-18).

> "However, if you suffer as a Christian, do not be ashamed, but praise God that you bear that name" (1Peter 4:16).

> "So then, those who suffer according to God's will should commit themselves to their faithful Creator and continue to do good" (1Peter 4:19).

Chapter 6

The Power of Submission

Submit yourselves, then, to God. Resist the devil, and he will flee from you. (James 4:7)

Submission is another sword with two edges. Submission that is forced is never pleasant or joyful. When I do something for someone and they say, "You didn't have to do that!" my response to them is, "If I had to do it, I wouldn't enjoy it near as much!" Submission to the Lord is exactly the same way. If we do it out of a sense of duty or guilt, it takes the joy out of it and it becomes very difficult and dreary. However, for those who have come to understand the joy that comes from serving Christ and submitting to His will, it is well worth every bump in the road.

Submission is just a recognition that God knows how to do things better than we do. Doings things His way is going to make my life more successful and I will enjoy it more. I have seen what I can do in my own methods, and frankly, I could use some help. The Bible is loaded with practical, useful, and helpful ways of seeing our world and going about our business. It is wisdom directly from the Creator. If anyone should know how to make life powerful and blessed, it is Him!

Submission is an indication that we trust the Lord to help us, shape us, protect us, and make our lives meaningful and fruitful. It recognizes that this life is short, and eternity is something worth spending our time here preparing for. If evil comes against me because of my stand for Christ, I trust that He will help me, deliver me, and teach me how to prevail for the sake of His glory. It is trusting that the Lord will not give us more than we can bear (1Corinthians 10:13).

I saw a sign on a church recently that said, "Ever been hurt because someone didn't trust you? Imagine how God feels." Our God has absolutely proven Himself to be a sacrificial giver. He gives for the sake of blessing others at His own very serious expense. "He who did not spare his own Son, but gave him up for us all--how will he not also, along with him, graciously give us all things" (Romans 8:32)? Submission to God is seeking what is good, and turning from the ways of the world. "Seek good, not evil, that you may live. Then the LORD God Almighty will be with you, just as you say he is" (Amos 5:14). The Lord's presence makes every attack, every loss, every rejection, every mocking comment of little concern or effect. You come to realize that all those things are specifically designed to back you away from the very thing that gives your life purpose and meaning. The people through whom they come generally have no idea what is going on. They are just reacting to something they sense inside. Something in you is causing friction with something in them. If we understand it, we will not take it as a personal affront. This is why Jesus said, "Father, forgive them, for they do not know what they are doing" (Luke 23:34).

> As for you, you were dead in your transgressions and sins, in which *you used to live when you followed the ways of this world and of the ruler of the kingdom of the air, the spirit who is now at work in those who are disobedient.* All of us also lived among them at one time, gratifying the cravings of our sinful nature and following its desires and thoughts. Like the rest, we were by nature objects of wrath (Ephesians 2:1-4, emphasis mine).

Submitting to the will of God does cause some trepidation, not only because of the fear of the unknown, but there are also many misconceptions out there concerning the will of God.

My wife feared that submission to the will of God was like a guaranteed one way ticket to the wilds of Africa or the jungles of Borneo to do missionary work. This held her back from a full, whole hearted commitment to the Lord's will for years. What we both came to understand through years of drawing near to Him was that He is not pushy and demanding, but patient and kind. His will is centered around your talents, gifts, and desires. What He wants you to do are things you *want* to do. Remember, He placed those desires and specific gifts in your heart for a reason. "Delight yourself in the LORD and he will give you the desires of your heart" (Psalms 37:4). Like any good parent, God wants His children to have the desires of their heart. He is also, however, a wise parent and He knows when those desires are properly centered.

Submitting to the Lord's will is an act of faith. Faith is "being confident of this, that he who began a good work in you will carry it on to completion until the day of Christ

Jesus" (Philippians 1:6). "And without faith it is impossible to please God, because anyone who comes to him must believe that he exists and that he rewards those who earnestly seek him" (Hebrews 11:6). ...rewards those who earnestly seek Him. What kind of rewards is the writer of Hebrews referring to here? I am not sure we even understand the array of blessings involved with this promise. Commanding His angels concerning us (Psalm 91)? I would think so. Fullness of the Spirit (Acts 13:52)? I am sure. How about answering our prayers? "The prayer of a righteous man is powerful and effective" (James 5:16).

Abraham's faith was credited to him as righteousness (Romans 4:9), and a standing before God as a righteous person opens many doors.

> "The righteous man is rescued from trouble, and it comes on the wicked instead" (Proverbs 11:9).

> "The righteous man leads a blameless life; blessed are his children after him" (Proverbs 20:7).

> "Surely he will never be shaken; a righteous man will be remembered forever" (Psalms 112:6).

"A righteous man may have many troubles, but the LORD delivers him from them all..." (Psalms 34:19).

When we are around people who just seem to be blessed; their prayers are being answered, they walk in love, and promote peace, you can bet that they have given themselves over to the will of God for their lives. They have invited the Savior to take over their lives and live out His life in them. They have asked the Lord to correct them and transform them into His image. They have asked the Lord to bring their gifts of the Spirit to the fore that they might be used in service to the Body of Christ. They have grasped the awesome power and amazing life for those who become servants of Christ. Their needs are taken care of; they are guided in the paths of righteousness; they are attentive to the will and the voice of the Spirit in their hearts; they lead lives filled with wonder and adventure, because the Lord loves to prove how trustworthy He is to those that would rest in Him. His yoke *is* easy, and His burden *is* light (Matthew 11:30).

Remember the two brothers who wanted to sit at Jesus' right and left in the Kingdom? "'You don't know what you are asking," Jesus said to them. "Can you drink the cup I am going to drink?" "We can," they answered (Matthew 20: 22). Could they have possibly known what they were saying? Looking back on it, what they said yes to seems outlandish, but Jesus then told them, "You will indeed drink from my cup, but to sit at my right or left is not for me to grant" (Matthew 20:23). Drinking from the Lord's cup; how does that sound? Challenging? Stretching? Life changing? Fraught with peril? Ultimately blessed? Would you like to try it? Want to think about it for a few minutes? Are any of us ready for that? I am just asking you to consider it for a few minutes. How "all in" are we?

Asking to drink from the cup may be on outer reaches of faith, but we can begin with submission to the Lord and His will for us as a practical step.

"Lord Jesus, I thank you for all that you have done, and all you continue to do in my life. I know that I can trust you to love me, guide me, transform me into your image, and deliver me safely into your loving arms when the time is right. I submit myself to you as my Lord, and ask you to take everything that is mine and make it yours. Everything I lose, I ask you to receive as an offering. I trust that I needed to let it go. Everything I gain, I accept with a humble heart and gracious thanksgiving to you. May it be used for the sake of your glory. Bless me, grant me the spirit of wisdom and revelation that I might know you better, and give me the ability to love others with your love. Help me to learn how to give like you give, and help me to overcome the world by your grace. In your holy and precious Name Savior. Amen."

> "I tell you the truth," Jesus replied, "no one who has left home or brothers or sisters or mother or father or children or fields for me and the gospel will fail to receive a hundred times as much in this present age (homes, brothers, sisters, mothers, children and fields--and with them, persecutions) and in the age to come, eternal life (Mark 10:29-30).

Chapter Seven

Speaking Parts

In his right hand he held seven stars, and out of his mouth came a sharp double-edged sword. His face was like the sun shining in all its brilliance (Revelation 1:16).

In the movie business, speaking parts are what everyone is after. They bring a person from the background as an extra to a place of importance in the story. A speaking part brings in more money, and the influence of the words that are spoken are forever integral to the lasting effect of the film.

There is no doubt that words convey power. The ability to form and speak words is what separates us from the rest of the animal kingdom. The Bible tells us that, "The tongue has the power of life and death, and those who love it will eat its fruit" (Proverbs 18:21). Life and death – can it get any more serious than that? "For by your words you will be acquitted, and by your words you will be condemned"

(Matthew 12:37). Most of us are completely unaware of the minefield we lay around us with the words we speak.

Please take a moment and consider a small sampling of what the Bible says about the power of words and the tongue:

> And the words of the LORD are flawless, like silver refined in a furnace of clay, purified seven times (Psalms 12:6).
>
> May the words of my mouth and the meditation of my heart be pleasing in your sight, O LORD, my Rock and my Redeemer (Psalms 19:14).
>
> ...keep your tongue from evil and your lips from speaking lies (Psalms 34:13).
>
> The words of his mouth are wicked and deceitful; he has ceased to be wise and to do good (Psalms 36:3).
>
> The mouth of the righteous man utters wisdom, and his tongue speaks what is just (Psalms 37:30).
>
> I will watch my ways and keep my tongue from sin; I will put a muzzle on my mouth as long as the wicked are in my presence (Psalms 39:1).
>
> They sharpen their tongues like swords and aim their words like deadly arrows (Psalms 64:3).

How sweet are your words to my taste, sweeter than honey to my mouth! (Psalms 119:103).

Before a word is on my tongue you know it completely, O LORD (Psalms 139:4).

Wisdom will save you from the ways of wicked men, from men whose words are perverse... (Proverbs 2:12).

It will save you also from the adulteress, from the wayward wife with her seductive words... (Proverbs 2:16).

...if you have been trapped by what you said, ensnared by the words of your mouth... (Proverbs 6:2).

When words are many, sin is not absent, but he who holds his tongue is wise (Proverbs 10:19).

The words of the wicked lie in wait for blood, but the speech of the upright rescues them (Proverbs 12:6).

Reckless words pierce like a sword, but the tongue of the wise brings healing (Proverbs 12:18).

Pleasant words are a honeycomb, sweet to the soul and healing to the bones (Proverbs 16:24).

The words of a man's mouth are deep waters, but the fountain of wisdom is a bubbling brook (Proverbs 18:4).

A fortune made by a lying tongue is a fleeting vapor and a deadly snare (Proverbs 21:6).

He who guards his mouth and his tongue keeps himself from calamity (Proverbs 21:23).

Through patience a ruler can be persuaded, and a gentle tongue can break a bone [!] (Proverbs 25:15).

The power and responsibility of the words we speak is something that is rarely focused on or highlighted in our Christian faith, but the Bible is loaded with warnings about the words we speak and the consequences of those words, not only for ourselves, but also for those to whom the words are directed. When one begins to understand the power and lasting effect of the words we speak, and you listen to the way people talk to each other, especially the words directed toward our children - the most vulnerable among us - it causes one to cringe inside. The Book of James tells us, "If anyone is never at fault in what he says, he is a perfect man, able to keep his whole body in check" (Chapter 3, Verse 2).

The power and significance of words is difficult to overstate. Now, for a moment, imagine the awesome power of *God's* words. "Heaven and earth will pass away, but my words will never pass away" (Matthew 24:35).

> As the rain and the snow come down from heaven, and do not return to it without watering the earth and making it bud and flourish, so that it yields seed for the sower and bread for the eater, so is my word that goes out from my mouth: It will not return to me empty, but will accomplish what I desire and achieve the purpose for which I sent it (Isaiah 55:10-11).

The Word of God has awesome power to manifest what God intends for it to accomplish. God's words are not just words on a page.

> For the word of God is living and active. Sharper than any double-edged sword, it penetrates even to dividing soul and spirit, joints and marrow; it judges the thoughts and attitudes of the heart (Hebrews 4:12).

Jesus, as we know, is the Word of God made flesh (John 1:14). Jesus made an interesting statement about the words that He spoke: "The Spirit gives life; the flesh counts for nothing. *The words I have spoken to you are spirit and they are life* (John 6:63, emphasis mine). Jesus was referring to His declaration that He was the "bread of life," but in my view, the same could be said for all of God's words; they are spirit and they are life, because God is a spirit and His Word sustains us and gives us life (John 1:4).

For us, as believers, the question becomes "How can I get the power of God's Word off of the pages of the book and into *my* life?" We certainly can read it and store it in our hearts. We can hear the Word of God preached and be edified by it. There are times, however, when the Word that resides inside needs to be manifest in our particular circumstances. Does speaking the Word of God activate it in our circumstances? Words have power; God's words have His power. "...so is my word *that goes out from my mouth*: It will not return to me empty, but will accomplish what I desire and achieve the purpose for which I sent it" (Isaiah 55:11, emphasis mine). God spoke and the light appeared (Genesis 1:3). Jesus spoke to the storm, and it was calmed (Mark 4:39). Jesus spoke to the fig tree, and it died! (Mark 11:20-21). Of course, we do not want things to die, except the power of the flesh; we want good to come.

We want to have what the Word of God says we can have and we want the blessings that the Word promises. We want them to be activated in our circumstances.

For example, there was a period of time in my life that I drove a taxi. For someone who enjoys interacting with people, this is a great job. You can be friendly, helpful, and make a few dollars as well. The city I was working in, however, had its rough areas and without the partition in the middle between the front and rear seats, one can feel quite vulnerable when questionable characters take a seat in the back. The old flesh tries to go a little crazy with the fears and concerns about what could happen. "I thank you Lord, that you have not given me a spirit of fear, but a spirit of power, of love, and a sound mind." I just spoke the Word over my circumstances as a prayer. "I know, Lord, that nothing shall in any way harm me" (Luke 10:19). This is Isaiah 52:12, "But you will not leave in haste or go in flight; for the LORD will go before you, the God of Israel will be your rear guard." "I thank you Lord for being my rear guard." My body seems to have a physiological response to these words. I start to relax. My breathing is more regular. It is amazing how many circumstances of life to which Scriptures apply.

Do I have to have a seminary degree to remember all these Scriptures? No, but reading the Word and storing them in your heart is a great help. The Spirit brings them to your remembrance as they become necessary. You will be amazed at the Word that is hidden there that you forgot completely about until you need it and it comes into your heart by God's grace. You can think those words and meditate on them, but it is more powerful to speak them or at least form the words on your lips. "Pay attention and listen to the sayings of the wise; apply your heart to what I teach, for it is pleasing when you keep them in your heart and have all of them ready on your lips" (Proverbs 22:17-18). This is a privilege reserved for God's people, "But to the wicked, God says: "What right have you to recite my laws or take my covenant on your lips" (Psalms 50: 16)?

God's Word is truth (John 17:17). Anything contradictory to that truth is a lie. My wife asked me once, "If Jesus took stripes on His back for believers to be healed, why do any Christians ever get sick?" I think she spends her free time coming up with stuff like this.

That is, however, a great question. The Word says that, "By His wounds we are healed" (Isaiah 53:5), and that, "He himself bore our sins in his body on the tree, so that we might die to sins and live for righteousness; by his wounds you have been healed" (1Peter 2:24). If sickness tries to manifest in your body, it is trying to contradict what is true in you. What should we do? You undoubtedly realize that there is a liar and deceiver loose in the world we live in. We do not live in a world of truth until a lie is told. That went away in the Garden of Eden. It will not be that way again until the Evil One is bound for the thousand years. We live in a world of lies until the truth is told.

Every lie is destroyed by the revelation of truth. A lie, unchallenged by truth, will continue to stand. We *can* contradict this lie by confessing the truth that the Word says concerning us: "Thank you Lord that by your stripes I was healed." "I know, Savior, that you have carried my sickness and disease, and taken up all my infirmities." "Thank you, Father that you sent your Word and healed us" (Psalm 107:20). It is not the chapter and verse that does the job; it is the truth in that verse being spoken in faith.

The Bible tells us that the truth of any matter is established by two or three witnesses (Deuteronomy 13:15). God's Word is His witness concerning Himself and what He has done for His people. When I pray those Scriptures in faith and with a thankful heart, I feel a manifestation of God's love after a minute or two (depending on the seriousness of what is happening) and feel better; completely healed by God's grace and love!

Sometimes we must persist in our confession, because these things do not always let go easily, but your persistent faith will pay off. Just keep speaking the truth. That lie will have to submit to it. The truth is way more powerful than any lie. The Lord does these things out of His love for us and for the sake of His glory. He told us through the Apostle Paul that, "It is for freedom that Christ has set us free" (Galatians 5:1) Please make sure that you give Him thanks when he delivers you from sickness or anything else, for that matter:

> One of them, when he saw he was healed, came back, praising God in a loud voice. He threw himself at Jesus' feet and thanked him--and he was a Samaritan. Jesus asked, "Were not all ten cleansed? Where are the other nine? Was no one

found to return and give praise to God except this foreigner?" (Luke 17:15-18)

Neither my wife nor I have been to a doctor in years. As the specter of socialized medicine looms, an appointment with the Great Physician may become the first choice for God's people. I am not saying that doctor's have no place in the Kingdom of God as we reside in this world. They are for the sick (Mark 2:17). I am the healed, in Jesus' Name!

Does this method work when it comes to spiritual warfare? You can bet that it does! "Thank you Lord, that greater is He that is in me, than he that is in the world, in your Holy Name" (1John 4:4). "I know Lord, that if I resist the devil, he shall flee from me (James 4:7), for your Name's sake." "No weapon forged against me will prosper (Isaiah 54:17), in Jesus' Name."

The Bible is loaded with Scriptures that are designed to give your testimony power to overcome. Remember, "They overcame him by the blood of the Lamb and by *the word* of their testimony…" (Revelation 12:11a, emphasis mine). Your testimony needs the Word in it so that you can have the power to prevail.

The applications here are endless. There are Scriptures for your children, your parents, your boss, and your co-workers, homes, neighbors, plants, life, health... You can speak God's Word over all your areas of concern to bless them. Remember though, that Jesus is a cornerstone for some, but a stumbling block for others (1Peter 2:7-8). Speaking the Word over some individuals may cause them problems. You will have to seek the Lord for wisdom.

You can speak Words of strength, life, deliverance, victory, peace, joy, wholeness, wellness, and freedom. The challenging thing is to find Scripture that applies to your circumstances. One resource that I find very helpful is blueletterbible.org.

Speak the truth in love and in the glory of the Savior, and you will bask in the freedom that truth brings!

Chapter Eight

Swordplay

Do not suppose that I have come to bring peace to the earth. I did not come to bring peace, but a sword (Matthew 10:34).

The first thing one needs to know about spiritual warfare is that it is a rigged endeavor. Jesus is the head of every principality and power (Colossians 2:10, NKJV). Since Jesus is our Lord, we can rest in Him, knowing that we will be all right, no matter what comes. Does that mean that nothing bad can happen? I did not say that! Remember, faith is an interactive effort. We have a part, and He has a part. If we do our part, He will definitely do His. Our job is to discover what our part is and do it:

> "Not everyone who says to me, 'Lord, Lord,' will enter the kingdom of heaven, but only he who does the will of my Father who is in heaven. Many will say to me on that day, 'Lord, Lord, did we not prophesy in your name, and in your name drive out demons and perform many miracles?' Then I will tell them plainly, 'I never

knew you. Away from me, you evildoers!'
"Therefore everyone who hears these words of mine and puts them into practice is like a wise man who built his house on the rock. The rain came down, the streams rose, and the winds blew and beat against that house; yet it did not fall, because it had its foundation on the rock. But everyone who hears these words of mine and does not put them into practice is like a foolish man who built his house on sand. The rain came down, the streams rose, and the winds blew and beat against that house, and it fell with a great crash" (Matthew 7:21-27).

Do the stakes get any higher than this? I cannot imagine how they *could* get any higher. There is a lot in this passage, but I would like to start with this: the people that Jesus is referring to here are doing many things in the Name of Christ. One of them is driving out demons. Is the modern church doing that? If they are not, I wonder if they have even reached this level of faith Jesus is describing in those He turns away.

You notice He did not have to inform the first century Jewish people that evil existed in the form of evil spirits. They told *Him* about it! It was a societal given. Demoniacs were all around them. Ever hear people today talking about "battling their demons?" The world has not changed. Society knows what is happening.

The Pharisees accused Jesus of using demonic power to drive out evil spirits. Jesus responded: "And if I drive out demons by Beelzebub, by whom do your people drive them out" (Matthew 12:27)? He also said that the righteousness of believers would have to surpass that of the Pharisees or else they would not enter the Kingdom of Heaven (Matthew 5:20). If the Pharisees were driving out evil spirits, and the modern church does not, where does that place us on the scale of righteousness - above the Pharisees or below them?

My point here is not to point the finger at the church; it is to point out the reality that the world is suffering in the grip of darkness. Should not the Church of Jesus Christ have some answers that include a conception of how to prevail in the realm of the spirit?

The difference between the two men described in Matthew 7:21-27 above is that one not only heard the words of the Savior, he put them into practice. He incorporated what he heard into his way of doing things. We know that Jesus is the Word of God; so as we read the

Word of God, it would be helpful to accept what it says and look for practical ways to do what is described; especially if it specifically says to do so. One place where we are instructed to do something is in Ephesians:

> Finally, be strong in the Lord and in his mighty power. *Put on* the full armor of God so that you can take your stand against the devil's schemes. For our struggle is not against flesh and blood, but against the rulers, against the authorities, against the powers of this dark world and against the spiritual forces of evil in the heavenly realms. Therefore put on the full armor of God, so that when the day of evil comes, you may be able to stand your ground, and after you have done everything, to stand (Ephesians 6:10-13, emphasis mine).

Our war is not against flesh and blood; it is against darkness embodied by "the spiritual forces of evil in the heavenly realms." Is the Bible referring to evil spirits? I believe that it is. Whatever it is, we do have instructions on how to deal with it here and other places in the Bible. We are instructed twice in this passage to "put on the full armor of God." When the Bible repeats itself like this, most scholars agree that it is to emphasize what is being said.

So, what are we being asked to do in this instance? We are asked to put God's Armor on. So now, how do we put in on? In prayer and by faith. Right after this passage, the pieces of the Armor are described:

- The sandals of peace, which is the Gospel of Christ.
- The girdle of truth.
- The breastplate of righteousness.
- The helmet of salvation.
- The shield of faith, with which we may extinguish all the fiery darts of the enemy.
- The sword of the Spirit, which is the Word of God.

This list is how I memorized it, because it was easier for me to remember them from the ground up. I may have a little New King James Version mixed up in there as well, but it works.

God is a spirit and He is invisible, so it makes sense that His Armor is invisible and spiritual also. Every day, I pray it on piece by piece in faith. I pray it on myself and my family; wife, children, grandchildren, and believing friends as the Lord directs. Please do not pray this onto anyone who is not a believer. They will have a struggle that they will not know how to deal with.

When you first start doing this, hang on for a storm, because evil will try to discourage you from "dressing" this way. People around you may have a major struggle and may lash out at you, having no idea why. The realm of the spirit in your immediate vicinity is getting stirred up because of the presence of something divine. It is because you are wearing something that is not yours. It is *God's* Armor. Can you try to wrap your understanding around the magnitude of that little setup? Did you ever like to dress up in your Dad's clothes as a kid? It made you feel all grown up. Putting on the Armor is like that times a million. You will get the craziest looks from people.

Things will settle down as everyone gets used to what is happening. For the loved ones who do not understand what is happening, try to encourage them that you are doing what the Bible tells you to do and that it will be all right. Ask them to join you, as long as they are Christians. Even if you have prayed it on them, it is more powerful for them to do it themselves. If you can manage to put on the

Armor for ten days in a row, I wager you will not miss a day the rest of your life. It is *that* big of a deal.

Will evil launch fiery darts at you? You can bet on it! But you can call on the "Shield of Faith" to extinguish them. "I thank you Lord that by the Shield of Faith, I extinguish every fiery dart of the enemy, in Jesus' Name." You will love "frustrating the schemes of the wicked" (Psalms 146:9). It is very gratifying. Those first ten days will be the most interesting. After that, if you forget to put it on, you will remember when things are going a little crazy. All of a sudden you realize; I forgot to put the Armor on!

The importance of this little bit of obedience cannot be overstated. Without this gift, you have no shot at overcoming anything. Can you imagine a modern football player going out on the field without his pads? What is going to happen to him? He will not accomplish a thing, except to have his hat handed to him, so to speak. He may have some bumps and bruises for his trouble - maybe worse. This is also true of any believer who tries to make a stand against evil without God's Armor. That is why He gave it to us; so we can prevail against the schemes of the devil.

Being "dressed for success" does not by itself guarantee success, but at least you are ready to step into the arena with the wherewithal to withstand the pushback caused by your efforts. You still have to make your stand with the Sword, but even if you lose your footing in a moment of weakness, the Armor will still keep you from being overwhelmed.

Are believers prepared to overcome the lie of darkness with the light of truth in Christ? The Lord tells us in many ways that the foundation has been laid, "I have given you authority to trample on snakes and scorpions and to overcome all the power of the enemy; nothing will harm you" (Luke 10:19). He is placing the power of darkness under the feet of believers for His Name's sake. One might pray, "I thank you Lord, that you have given me authority to trample on serpents and scorpions. I command the power of darkness around me to get under my feet, in Jesus' Holy Name."

> Let the saints rejoice in this honor and sing for
> joy on their beds. May the praise of God be in
> their mouths and a double-edged sword in their

hands, to inflict vengeance on the nations and punishment on the peoples, to bind their kings with fetters, their nobles with shackles of iron, to carry out the sentence written against them. This is the glory of all his saints. Praise the LORD (Psalms 149:5-9).

This, my friends, *is* an honor *and* a privilege. Please ask the Savior to grant you wisdom in this blessing and help you see your role in this amazing ministry. "I bind those kings with fetters, Lord, those nobles with shackles of iron, in Your Holy Name."

From my view, the binding of their kings with fetters and the nobles with shackles is how vengeance and punishment occur in the "nations." "Nations" in the Old Testament referred to unbelieving or pagan nationalities. In our modern view, it refers to unbelievers, according to many. For those who count on the power of darkness as their source of inspiration, their anchor is taken away. The power and love of Christ now seems more viable to them. If the darkness that unbelievers call on is getting bound by the authority of Christ, the glory of the Gospel shines even brighter because there is that much less darkness trying to slow it down and oppose it.

Most people who are bound by darkness are there because they fear the power of it. When they see the glory of Christ prevailing over that evil, they will be more willing to step into the light to bask in its love and warmth. We know that the Lord is really in charge and we have nothing to fear, as long as we keep walking in the light.

Now, back to the two men in Matthew 7 who faced the driving rain, rising waters, and fierce winds. One was anchored to the Rock and one was not. They both faced the same storms, but the outcomes were different. Of course, Jesus is our Rock. How do we remain anchored to Him?

For one thing, we need to know *what* the Word says to be able to *do* what it says. "Now I commit you to God and to the word of his grace, which can build you up and give you an inheritance among all those who are sanctified" (Acts 20:32). These were Paul's words to the church at Ephesus, and they are still true for us today. The Word of God does build us up. Those words are spirit and life (John 6:63). We need to ingest some of the Word every day to gird us for our daily grind.

"Five of you will chase a hundred, and a hundred of you will chase ten thousand, and your enemies will fall by the sword before you" (Leviticus 26:8). In the times of the Old Testament, Israel's enemies were real people who wanted to kill them. I guess *that* has not changed! What has changed for Christians are the methods of dealing with our enemies. The battle is now in the realm of the spirit, not against flesh and blood; so now, wielding the sword is done by speaking truth (God's Word) over circumstances. The Sword of the Spirit is the Word of God.

> The weapons we fight with are not the weapons of the world. On the contrary, they have divine power to demolish strongholds. We demolish arguments and every pretension that sets itself up against the knowledge of God, and we take captive every thought to make it obedient to Christ. And we will be ready to punish every act of disobedience, once your obedience is complete (2Corinthians 10:4-6).

This is another tightly packed bit of Scripture. The weapons described here have divine power - God's power. Now we have God's Armor and God's power to demolish strongholds. Strongholds used to be made of stone. According to this passage, they are, in this context, perversions of truth specifically designed to keep people from knowing God. A pretense is something that one knows is not true. They are just pretending. Is there some kind of malevolent force in our world that is trying to keep people from knowing God and His truth? Oh, right – evil.

So if evil basically works for God to punish mankind for the disobedience of Adam, and Jesus came into the world to destroy the works of the devil (1John 3:8), why do believers have to use the divine power of these weapons and put on the Armor to destroy these strongholds so the knowledge of God is not impeded by twisted assertions?

Well, maybe we are being given a chance to walk by faith, learn obedience, and come to grips with the reality of the spirit realm. Maybe this is the consequence of Adam's partaking of the fruit. We now know and have to deal with the knowledge of good and evil. God is giving us an opportunity to stand for truth and stand in the gap for the lost. He is developing our faith and using these obstacles to grow us up and transform our thinking. He is sharing His victory with us! If those strongholds *are* broken down, the knowledge of God is more evident to the lost. The Gospel becomes more powerful in the hearts of the unconverted.

There are a couple more things that are resident in the Scripture about our warfare in 2Corinthians. One is that the battlefield is in the mind. "...we take captive every thought to make it obedient to Christ" (verse 5b). The difference between cleanliness and uncleanness is in our thoughts:

> Don't you see that whatever enters the mouth goes into the stomach and then out of the body? But the things that come out of the mouth come from the heart, and these make a man 'unclean.' *For out of the heart come evil thoughts*, murder, adultery, sexual immorality, theft, false testimony, slander. These are what make a man 'unclean'; but eating with unwashed hands does not make him 'unclean' (Matthew 15:17-20, emphasis added).

Keeping our thoughts in check protects us from uncleanness and prevents the power of our weapons from being undermined by sin. Evil knows how to insert thoughts into our minds. Our job is to reject those thoughts and make them captive.

One pastor said, concerning thoughts that suddenly appear in our mind: "It is like a bird that flies by; we cannot stop them from buzzing us, but we do not have to allow them to build a nest in our hair either."

One lady related to me how she was haunted by thoughts of killing her daughter when her daughter was just a toddler. She was so horrified by those thoughts that she went to see a psychologist out of fear of doing something awful. You can imagine the outcome, right? Her daughter was taken from her and she was committed for 72 hours of observation. Afterward, she went on a long odyssey of powerful psychotropic drugs and state care. Her daughter never again lived with her and resents what happened to this day.

Did anyone understand what was happening to this dear lady? These stories are so tragic and awful, yet not so uncommon. God's people have to be able to come in and say, "We can deal with this in the Name of our Lord." Could she have taken her concerns to her church? Would they have known what to do?

Thoughts must be taken captive and made obedient. The Blood of the Lamb and the anointing of Christ were needed. She needed the Word of God to build up her defenses. The truth could have definitely overcome that lie. Lives, and the quality of those lives are at stake!

"And we will be ready to punish every act of disobedience, once your obedience is complete" (2Corinthians 10:6). Now this is a powerful statement! What is being said here? *Our* obedience has a direct and highly desirable benefit. Do we want God to punish disobedience? We certainly do! But why does it depend on us? We are already saved! Ahh, but this is an incentive to grow up. This is an incentive to trust God and prevail in His Name. If God's people are not willing to do *their* part, evil in those who are evil will not be punished. If it is not punished, our world continues to degrade. Please recall this passage from 2Chronicles 7:14: "...if my people, who are called by my name, will humble themselves and pray and seek my face and turn from their wicked ways, then will I hear from heaven and will forgive their sin and will heal their land." Is the world the way it is because of the evil in it, or because God's people are unable or unwilling to do their part, or both? The Scripture is telling us what needs to happen. If we do our part, we know that He will do His!

Wielding the Sword of Truth has a myriad of applications. We need the Lord's wisdom to know what is going on and how to deal with it. One way believers can seek the Lord's input into their circumstances is to pick up their Bible and just open it, trusting the Holy Spirit to guide them to the right place. I started doing this by "accident." I would pick up my Bible and open it to look for something, and I would just glance at the place where it happened to open. What I was reading was incredibly relevant to what I was going through. I started doing it all the time. I found the Lord guiding me to some places that opened up new vistas of faith for me. There were revelations about who He was and the things He was looking for in us. Sometimes there were passages that He would use to "quicken" my heart. I would start studying and meditating on those passages, allowing them to permeate my soul.

Honestly, most of what is written in this book is due to the things that He had me open to in the Word, helping me make connections in the Scripture to things that may have never been made otherwise. Sometimes the things I opened to were passages that I would speak over my circumstances, seeing immediate, powerful, and much needed results.

Not everyone recommends this method. I heard R.C. Sproul call this "lucky dipping" on his radio show years ago. He did relate how a young student of his had tried this method concerning a man she was contemplating marrying and the Word had encouraged her, so she went ahead, feeling good about it, sensing the Lord's endorsement in the Word to which she opened. He did say she was doing well last he had heard.

I also heard Benny Hinn say that he does it sometimes, but is scared to death he might open to some passage of severe judgment, with God saying he would die. That has actually happened to me. I asked the Lord if the Word I opened to pertained to me and if there was something for which I needed to repent. There was. I did. Afterward, I opened to more pleasant things. The message, however, did get through.

Not everything we open to will be directly about us. It may have to do with something going on around us. We can ask the Lord, "Is this about me, Lord?" "Is this a picture of my attitude or actions?" "Is this something that I need to be aware of in my circle?" Spiritual discernment is really important here. Seek wisdom concerning the things you open to and the Lord emphasizes by His "quickening."

There is an amazing story about this practice that happened in the fourth century. Have you heard of St. Augustine? He was an early church father and a bishop in North Africa. We still use much of his theological views in our modern practice of faith.

He was schooled in "rhetoric." This was the degree that attorneys back in that day wanted to establish their careers. As it turned out, he worked for the Roman government as a herald. He would go from town to town and read the decrees of the government to the peoples of each village. This was a very important and highly sought after job. Family connections had to be used to get a job like that.

Problem was, he was torn between his career as a herald and the call he felt to serve the Lord. It was a classic tug-of-war in his heart. He had worked long and hard to get where he was in his career, but his heart was in ministry. The struggle intensified, and Augustine would take time off to go to out-of-the-way places to pray and seek the Lord.

One day, he was in the walled garden area of the house he was renting. His heart was in agony, and he cried out to the Lord for help. He was actually weeping and broken because of the internal angst that was ripping him up inside. He said that he heard the voice of what sounded like a small child from somewhere over the wall. It said, "Take up and read. Take up and read." His Bible was right next to him on a bench. He picked it up and opened it. What he opened to changed his life forever. It was the Words of Christ during His time of temptation in the desert: "Worship the Lord your God and serve Him only" (Matthew 4:10). The impact of those words on Augustine's life was like a sledgehammer. He knew what God was calling him to do and he would do it! It was now crystal clear. He quit his job immediately and began his ministry. He founded monasteries and trained many future Christian leaders. He became a bishop and wrote many books on the faith and against heresies of the day. The Word of God changed his life. It is designed to have that kind of practical impact in all of our lives.

When I was contemplating marriage for the second time, I did not want to make another mistake brought about by my ignorance to spiritual matters, so I asked the Lord to show me in the Word if this was the right woman. When I opened the Word, this is where my eyes landed: "He who finds a wife finds what is good and receives favor from the LORD" (Proverbs 18:22). It is not just that I opened to this, my heart felt really good about it also. This is the Lord "quickening" His Word. It is that soft, loving, peaceful feeling in the heart when you know something is right. This is in contrast to the tightening in the gut when you know something is just spiritually wrong. That kind of discernment needs to be developed by use and experience: "But solid food is for the mature, who by constant use have trained themselves to distinguish good from evil" (Hebrews 5:14). By the way, my wife and I just celebrated our 17th wedding anniversary and are doing very well, thank you! Thank you too, Lord!

One thing the believer *must* keep in mind is that our war is against darkness, not people. Sadly, however, people have embraced darkness in our world on a massive scale. They are either inundated with evil because they have been exposed to it in music, television, books, magazines, movies, or the internet and had no defense against it, or they are actively operating in what the Bible calls the "magic arts" (Revelation 9:21, 21:8). In either case, and it does not matter to the believer, dark powers seem to emanate from worldly people in varying degrees, whether they are actively involved or not.

For me, this is why Jesus told us to bless those who curse us and pray for those who persecute us (Matthew 5:44). It is a recognition that while the evil is bad, the people have been provided for in God's grace, if they would receive it. Jesus loved us *and* them, while we were still His enemies (Romans 5:10). We are recognizing that just because we have arrived ahead of them, it does not necessarily make us *better* than them. They can still repent and be welcomed into God's love. Blessing them and praying for them helps to promote this possibility.

It is, however, deeper than that. If God blesses them because of our prayer for them, He will treat them as His sons. God loves His sons and disciplines them, does He not (Deuteronomy 8:5, Proverbs 3:12, Hebrews 12:6)? It is one of the pervasive and enduring themes of the Bible. With the power of God's fatherly discipline at work, evil will no longer be a desirable endeavor. Repentance cannot be far behind. We have to trust that things will work out and you will be amazed at how powerful it is to pray for those who come against you in some way, be it physically or spiritually.

When someone has a bad reaction to you, and you know you did not invite it in any way, it must be spiritual friction. When that occurs, please realize that what they are really saying by their actions is that they are miserable; it upsets them that you seem so happy and content, and they wish you would pray for them because they desperately need it. This will help you have compassion for someone that really needs help, and you will be shocked at how they relax and feel a connection to you they could not explain. It is our Lord blessing you for your willingness to understand the circumstances and for not succumbing to a victim mindset.

> But I tell you: Love your enemies and pray for those who persecute you, that you may be sons of your Father in heaven. He causes his sun to rise on the evil and the good, and sends rain on the righteous and the unrighteous. If you love those who love you, what reward will you get? Are not even the tax collectors doing that? And if you greet only your brothers, what are you doing

more than others? Do not even pagans do that? Be perfect, therefore, as your heavenly Father is perfect (Matthew 5:44-48).

Chapter Nine

Unwrapping the Gifts

> And these signs will accompany those who believe: in my name they will cast out demons; they will speak in new tongues; they will pick up serpents with their hands; and if they drink any deadly poison, it will not hurt them; they will lay their hands on the sick, and they will recover (Mark 16:17-18, ESV).

There are many modern churches today that do not believe that healings and miracles continue to be available to the Body of Christ. Most of them think that the power to heal and deliver was limited to the first century apostles for the purpose of establishing Christianity. What shocks me the most is that they say it with real sincerity. Without the power to heal and deliver, the church is no more than a religious club. There is absolutely nothing wrong with a religious club; but what is troubling is that the members of those churches are being taught *not* to trust in the power of the Savior to heal and deliver them in their trials.

The Apostle Paul wrote to the churches he founded on the subject of healing, deliverance, and spiritual gifts. If it was going to end with him and the other apostles, it would make no sense for him to teach them about these subjects. Healing actually *is* one of the gifts of the Spirit (1Corinthians 12:9).

> All Scripture is God-breathed and is useful for teaching, rebuking, correcting and training in righteousness, so that the man of God may be thoroughly equipped for every good work (2Timothy 3:16).

The Word of God is still in effect, brothers and sisters, and anyone who tries to skirt the authority of the Word for their own purposes (and only the Lord knows what those are), will have to give an account to the Lord. Not only for their own actions and unwillingness to take a stand for truth, but for what was wrongly taught to those who were purchased by the Blood of Christ and attend the churches that assert that some of the New Testament is no longer applicable.

Jesus paid the price for their freedom. If anything is done to undermine the ability of the church member to walk in that freedom, I would not want to stand before the Savior and explain to Him why these people were dissuaded from trusting in the power of His Name. As Christian leaders and teachers, they will be judged more rigorously (James 3:1). "For the kingdom of God is not a matter of talk but of power" (1Corinthians 4:20).

> But mark this: There will be terrible times in the last days. People will be lovers of themselves, lovers of money, boastful, proud, abusive, disobedient to their parents, ungrateful, unholy, without love, unforgiving, slanderous, without self-control, brutal, not lovers of the good, treacherous, rash, conceited, lovers of pleasure rather than lovers of God-- *having a form of godliness but denying its power. Have nothing to do with them* (2Timothy 3:1-5, emphasis mine).

The fact of the matter is that the power of healing, deliverance, and divine love are still available to all who call upon the Name of the Lord. Please remember: it is Jesus, as the Word of God, seated at the right hand of the Father, the Head of everything that exists, that heals, delivers, and loves. *He* has not changed. His desire to see His people walk in His love and freedom has not changed ("It is for freedom that Christ has set us free" [Galatians 5:1]). As long as He remains who He is and where He is (Jesus Christ is the same yesterday and today and forever

[Hebrews 13:8]), His love for us, and His desire for us to walk in victory will not be altered.

Some will ask, "Why don't we see more miracles and major demonstrations of God's power?" That is a very fair question. The parting of the Red Sea was an act that was in response to a national crisis for a people who were acting in faith as a nation. How many nations today are calling on the Name of the Lord in a time of national crisis?

One might say that the American colonists were calling upon the Name of the Lord in their struggle against the British during the Revolutionary War. Our defeat of the British was an absolute miracle. There is no other way to explain how these few, underfunded, starving, and freezing men could outlast the planet's most formidable fighting force.

Our American Constitution is another national miracle for a people seeking to honor and serve the Lord in their conduct and governance. It is a simple and straightforward document that preserves freedom in amazing ways that could not have been foreseen by those who framed it. Those who would seek to undermine freedom hate our Constitution and do everything in their power to ignore it or subvert it. The godly men who framed this priceless document were seeking the Lord's help for the sake of this new Republic.

How about Israel and the Six Day War? *Six Day War*! Israel was surrounded by enemies more powerful than she; and they were determined to destroy her. This is a miracle that should be studied. It makes no logical sense that they could subdue those enemies and take the land they did with so few people in so little time. That was almost fifty years ago.

What nations are calling on the Name of the Lord today? In April 2009, in a state visit to Turkey, President Obama announced to the world that America is a post-Christian nation. "...when the Son of Man comes, will he find faith on the earth" (Luke 18:8)? Unless there is some faith remaining on a national scale, it would undoubtedly explain why so few big, dramatic miracles occur.

So where *do* miracles occur? Miracles happen in the lives of those who place their trust in the God of the Bible, and His Son, Jesus Christ. What is so amazing about our God is that He is so awesome and pervasive, yet incredibly and surgically delicate. Most miracles are immediately recognizable to those who have been seeking God and trusting the Lord for them, but others find them to be eminently explicable, apart from the miraculous. My wife and I look at each other sometimes over these things and sardonically say to one another, "Just another *giant* coincidence!" We *know* it is Him watching over His Word to perform it. We have spent our time looking at events and circumstances and looking for God's "fingerprints" in the things that happen. Once one begins to see the cause and effect relationships between faith and positive response, as opposed to that of fear and doubt bringing negative or no response, the reality begins to emerge.

I heard one person say that God does not respond to the passion or pitiful nature of our pleas for help, He responds to faith. This is not because God is indifferent to our needs; it is because He has already provided for them. When we cry, "God, please heal me!" – one can imagine the Lord saying, "I already did. Do you know that my Son Jesus took stripes on His back so that you *are* healed?" It is already done. We *were* healed – past tense (1Peter 2:24, NKJV). We *are* healed - present tense (Isaiah 53:5). These Scriptures assert what is already accomplished. What we need to do is receive that healing by faith. Jesus does not have to go back to the Cross every time an unbelieving person wants to be saved, nor does He have to take more stripes for our healing. We thank Him for what He has provided and do not let fear and doubts talk us out of it.

The truth in us must prevail over the lie of the flesh. There is no doubt that this can be like a death match at times. We can certainly ask the Lord to help us walk in the truth of His Word. He surely knows that we need Him for that. Thanking Him and praising Him for what He has already done in spite of the circumstances is the key. We walk by faith, not by sight (2Corinthians 5:7).

Now, there is another issue that must be addressed. Obedience is a major factor when seeking miraculous power.

> To the Jews who had believed him, Jesus said,
> "If you hold to my teaching, you are really my
> disciples. Then you will know the truth, and the
> truth will set you free" (John 8:31-32).

The love of God may be unconditional, but how about His promises; are they conditional? In the Bible, we are always looking for what we must do, as opposed to what God will do as a response. My part vs. His part. The words "if" and "unless" are called "conditional clauses." When we see one of those two words, we should be looking for the condition that needs to be met for the benefit that would result.

In this case (John 8:31-32), it is to "hold to my teaching." What teaching is He referring to here? Honestly, it does not say, but there are a few things we know. We should love our enemies, bless those who curse us, have faith in God, walk humbly with our God, submit to authority, honor our parents in the Lord, forgive others when they harm us, do not repay evil for evil, do not seek our own vengeance… you know, basic Ten Commandment kinds of things. If our Christian witness is being damaged by our actions, and the Lord would seem to be endorsing bad behavior by bringing miraculous power to the circumstances, it is possible that our efforts will be in vain. If we are in need, and nothing is happening as we rest in the truth, we can seek Him for wisdom.

> Test me, O LORD, and try me, examine my heart
> and my mind; for your love is ever before me,
> and I walk continually in your truth (Psalms 26:2-3).

> "I the LORD search the heart and examine the mind, to reward a man according to his conduct, according to what his deeds deserve" (Jeremiah 17:10).
>
> O LORD Almighty, you who examine the righteous and probe the heart and mind, let me see your vengeance upon them, for to you I have committed my cause (Jeremiah 20:12).
>
> Let us examine our ways and test them, and let us return to the LORD (Lamentations 3:40).

Lastly, and as we have discussed earlier, evil wants to oppose the miraculous power of healing and deliverance. This stuff might get out! Many believers become discouraged when they pray and nothing seems to happen. Remember, the opposition to truth is a spiritual war, and evil spirits are doing their best to enforce the lie, in whatever form it may exist. When we pray, and we are obedient, those spirits are bound. What happens is that more spirits show up, reinforcing their compatriots, and since they are invisible, we do not know anything occurred. As far as we know, nothing changed. This is when most people give up. What the Lord taught me to do, by His grace, is keep at it. They come in legions. It might sound like this: "I know Lord, that by your stripes I was healed. I also know that you have given me the keys to the kingdom, Lord. Whatsoever I bind on earth will be bound in heaven. I bind every foul spirit that would try to enforce this lie of sickness against me, in the Name of the Lord Jesus. I bind legion, after legion, after legion, after legion, after tens of legions, after hundreds of legions, after thousands of legions... in your Holy Name Lord." I keep going until I start to feel something start to give, then I stay there , at whatever level I was at numerically when I felt the change, and keep after it until whatever the issue was is completely gone. Then I make sure and give the Lord praise for His grace.

Also, do not forget that whatsoever we loose on earth will be loosed in heaven (Matthew 16:19). "Father, I know that whatsoever I loose on earth will be loosed in heaven. I loose wholeness, wellness, victory, and freedom over myself, in Jesus Name." We can certainly pray this way over others as well. Seeing results is great encouragement when we see the truth prevailing over the lie, and I pray that these practical pointers will serve you well in your fight for truth and victory in the love of Christ.

Our families, our churches, our communities, and our nation really need God's people to understand these issues and stand in the gap for those who need a hand bearing up under their burdens. Remember, "Though one may be overpowered, two can defend themselves. A cord of three strands is not quickly broken (Ecclesiastes 4:12). When things get tough and gritty, God's people can stand together by faith. Get two other strong praying people to agree with you in prayer. Your prayers will be extremely powerful and you will not be easily broken, in the Name of Jesus and by God's grace!

Chapter Ten

The Voice

My sheep listen to my voice; I know them, and they follow me (John 10:27).

Sheep are interesting animals. They definitely have a herd mentality. They tend to move and react to things as a group. One of the things that is fascinating about sheep is the relationship they have with their shepherds. Two shepherds can be walking with their flocks and stop for a conversation as they approach one another. Their sheep are naturally a little nervous and will stay behind their shepherd as this conversation takes place. After a few moments, they may or may not mingle with the flock of the other shepherd. When their own shepherd gives them the command to move, they will do so. The other sheep do not respond until their own shepherd gives them *his* command, whether they are intermingled or not. They will only respond to the voice of their own shepherd.

The shepherd, likewise, knows every one of his sheep. If something were to happen to one of them, it would be like a family member going through a trial. He would do everything in his power to make sure that sheep was properly cared for. If one of the sheep gets lost, he will not quit looking until it is found. He will protect his flock from any predatory force. If they become sick or wounded, he tenderly nurses them back to health. He applies a salve to their wounds and watches over his animal to make sure the wound heals properly.

A salve can be an ointment that heals or relieves the pain of wounds or sores. The word salvation comes from the same root Latin word. In the biblical context, it is the loving care of a Good Shepherd that knows His sheep, tends to their needs, calms their fears, and salves their wounds and discomfort with His anointed love. This is a close, intimate relationship, where both sides are aware of the other, and work together for a common goal.

That Jesus, our Shepherd, knows us is crucial. It is not just an awareness of one's existence, it is knowing in the "biblical sense" which implies intimacy and closeness, so that each party is able to communicate with the other and knows how the other feels. When Jesus says to those who assumed that they were doing God's work, "I never knew you. Away from me, you evildoers!" (Matthew 7:23), is He saying that they knew *of* Him, but did not know *Him*?

Imagine that there was a President that you really revered. He was in office and you followed his every move. You did extensive research on his life; you knew where he was born, who his parents were, something about his lineage, where he went to school, what he liked and disliked, all about his wife, kids, pets, everything there was to know about him that had been written or discussed. You felt like you knew him so well, you decided to go to the White House to see your hero.

You show up at the front gate and announce your desire to see the President. The front gate calls upstairs and they have no idea who you are. You know everything there is to know about him, but he knows nothing about you. You even did things that you knew he would like you to do, but that was not the point; no relationship had ever been established.

What about the inauguration? He was connected to me then because I am a citizen and that ceremony connected us, did it not? Formally, yes, but not in a *personal* way. The White House front gate would ask you politely to leave.

When we say the sinner's prayer, we *are* inaugurating a relationship, but relationships need to develop for both parties to really know one another. The amazing thing is that the Lord has given us the privilege of drawing near to Him.

> Therefore, brothers, since we have confidence to enter the Most Holy Place by the blood of Jesus, by a new and living way opened for us through the curtain, that is, his body, and since we have a great priest over the house of God, *let us draw near to God* with a sincere heart in full assurance of faith, having our hearts sprinkled to cleanse us from a guilty conscience and having our bodies washed with pure water (Hebrews 10:19-22, emphasis added).
>
> Come near to God and he will come near to you. Wash your hands, you sinners, and purify your hearts, you double-minded (James 4:8).

In my view, the message here is that God has made a tremendous move toward us by providing us access to Himself in Christ. Now, if we really desire to know Him, we can come; we can enter into His presence and learn His ways, foregoing the ways of the world. "Take my yoke upon you and *learn* from me, for I am gentle and humble in heart, and you will find rest for your souls" (Matthew 11:29, emphasis mine).

How is this done? First, like everything else in the Christian faith, we can ask the Lord for it. Giving voice to our desire to know His ways and learn from Him is a crucial first step. This is another place where discernment is critically important. That way, if we have a question about something, we can seek the Lord in our heart about it and gauge our hearts response; yea or nay - good sense or not so good. As was mentioned earlier, discernment needs to be developed.

One way to do this is to ask the Lord about things in which the answer is already known, just to get a sense of what a yes or no feels like. "Is the sky blue, Lord?" In your heart you say the opposites: the sky is blue; the sky is not blue, just to gauge the internal response to each assertion. He knows what you are doing and it will not be a problem.

My wife and I like to go on driving trips to do local sightseeing. One of the things we do to engage the Lord and develop discernment is to ask Him as we approach every intersection, "Left, right, or straight?" This has to be done quickly to keep from holding up traffic, but we have found the most amazing places doing this – places we know the Lord helped us discover by leading us in our enterprise of faith.

We even found a church this way once. I was working graveyard shift and could not make it to the regular service. We wanted to go to the Sunday night service. We were new to the church having just moved to the area. The church was closed when we arrived! They were meeting in homes. We did not know anyone well enough to know where any of these places were, and I was distraught. This was back when I was a newer believer, and my soul was crying out for the salve of God's presence we knew would be in the worship service. I was craving His rejuvenating Spirit!

We were out in a rural area and we started looking for other churches nearby. We found another one, but the building had been sold and the congregation had moved on. No forwarding address! This was not going well, to say the least. We asked the Lord to guide us, and started seeking Him at the intersections. We ended up further out in the country and felt led to turn down a street that looked like it was lined with small acreages and what we call "gentlemen farms." Down that rural street was a church that was about twenty minutes into their Sunday night service. What a blessing! It turned out to be the group who had sold their building and moved to this new location. They did not have any signs up yet, but the Lord guided us right there. We stayed there for many years and I became a deacon in the church, enjoying God's grace. We were so thankful for God's goodness!

All that is wonderful, but one needs to be cautious as well: "... for Satan himself masquerades as an angel of light" (2Corinthians 11:14). We must "test the spirits" to make sure they are from God, or we may be taken on a wild goose chase that could take some serious grace from which to recover.

> "Dear friends, do not believe every spirit, but test the spirits to see whether they are from God, because many false prophets have gone out into the world. This is how you can recognize the Spirit of God: Every spirit that acknowledges that Jesus Christ has come in the flesh is from God, but every spirit that does not acknowledge Jesus is not from God.

This is the spirit of the antichrist, which you
have heard is coming and even now is already
in the world" (1John 4:1-3).

The question, then, must be posed, and the result must be discerned internally. "Has Jesus Christ come in the flesh?" Yea or nay? Good sense or not so good. This is the gold standard by which every other sensation should be judged. One can compare the sensation received from the issue of concern against this test question. If the sense is the same, it is a good indication. If there is uncertainty, revisit the issue more than once and ask the Lord to help you know His will.

Everything that one senses must also square with the Word of God. It can never be contradictory to the Word. If you sense that there is a conflict, the Word as written should be followed and everything else re-evaluated. The Lord deserves some credit here. He knows what you are doing, and He will not let you get too far afield if your motives are right.

Before making any earth shattering decisions based on your senses, ask the Lord to confirm it in the Word; then open up the Word and see what He says. I also ask my wife to seek the Lord on the same subject and give me her objective sense of things. We need to make it more about what *He* wants, instead of what *we* want. He does know best, and seeking His will for us is a great idea! Of course, my wife also has to agree to what we are proposing. If she has deep concerns about it, and I know in my heart it is God's will, I will wait for the Lord to comfort her. As long as it really *is* His will, I trust Him to calm her fears and for her to be a willing participant. Otherwise, some resentment may mar the process.

If my wife and I are both sensing the same thing from the Lord, I am about 99% sure we have it right. If it is a *really* big decision, I will ask someone else I trust that hears from the Lord and ask them to pray about it as well. If we all three agree, and my heart still feels good about it, I am certain that what we heard was a "God thing." We start making our plans and trust Him that His will is being done. We should stay in touch with the Lord to make sure nothing changes, but otherwise, go ahead and make things happen.

> Dear friends, if our hearts do not condemn us, we have confidence before God and receive from him anything we ask, because we obey his commands and do what pleases him (1John 3:22).

I quit a six figure a year job with ultimate security to go back to school and enter into ministry. We needed the Lord's assurance it was Him guiding us in that direction because everyone else thought we were nuts. We used the method described and were quite sure it was Him. It has been an amazing adventure in the years since. I am not that concerned if everyone else agrees it was a good thing, we knew in our hearts it was Him, and a third person we trusted heard the same thing, so away we went!

In a relationship, it is crucial for both sides to have an input. Certainly the Lord is willing to listen to us and hear our prayers, questions, and concerns about faith, the Bible, our relationship to Him, or anything else that troubles us. What about us hearing Him in our hearts? Is that possible? The Lord does not benefit from hearing us like we would benefit from hearing Him!

> "Man does not live on bread alone, but on every word that comes from the mouth of God" (Deuteronomy 8:3, Matthew 4:4).

> "The Sovereign LORD has given me an instructed tongue, to know the word that sustains the weary. He wakens me morning by morning, wakens my ear to listen like one being taught" (Isaiah 50:4).

In Matthew 4:4, the Greek term for "word" that comes from the mouth of God is rhema, or the inspired word, the word uttered by the "living voice." If we seek the Lord for this grace, we can wake up in the morning, be "still" before the Lord, and seek a "word" from Him in our spirit. This is another thing that will develop over time. The challenge is to get our thoughts quieted and find that "quiet place" to wait on the Lord. The word or phrase will come into your heart; it is heard with spiritual "ears." We must have the Spirit alive in us for it to be received. Certainly, make sure it is a valid Word by the means we have already discussed, but otherwise meditate on it and let it encourage you over the course of the day. It really does make mornings incredibly blessed and exciting to anticipate!

Hearing from the Lord is the greatest assurance that we are in good stead with Him and that He is being glorified in our lives. He wants us to hear from Him so that we can be even more built up in our faith, and assured of His love.

Chapter Eleven

Our Daily Bread

My heart is stirred by a noble theme as I recite my verses for the king... (Psalms 45:1a).

Jesus told us that He is the Bread of Life (John 6:35). What does that mean to us today? Does He understand the needs we have in this day and age? Are they the same as they were back in ancient times? These are questions that I had for the Lord in my own search for truth when it came to life issues.

I was going through a bad break up from the mother of my two girls and was struggling mightily. I thought I was getting by all right until I heard one of my supervisors at work saying to another supervisor about me, "If you stay back a ways, you can't see how bad his hands are shaking." That was eye opening! Not exactly a "high point" for me. I did not just *want* to know the Lord and His mercy; I *needed* it. I was not sure, however, if we were still talking about the same things. I cried out to the Lord for help and wisdom about this "bread of life" concept. How could *I* have it? He led me to the Book of John:

> Jesus said to them, "I tell you the truth, unless you eat the flesh of the Son of Man and drink his blood, you have no life in you. Whoever eats my flesh and drinks my blood has eternal life, and I will raise him up at the last day. For my flesh is real food and my blood is real drink. Whoever eats my flesh and drinks my blood remains in me, and I in him. Just as the living Father sent me and I live because of the Father, so the one who feeds on me will live because of me. This is the bread that came down from heaven. Your forefathers ate manna and died, but he who feeds on this bread will live forever" (John 6:53-58).

There is some amazing truth in this passage concerning life. Can you imagine what the crowds and the followers of Christ thought about this as He was standing before them declaring it? It sounds a little crazy - bizarre, cultish. As a matter of fact, most everyone walked away from Him except the Twelve because of this statement. He *did* go on to explain to the Twelve that it was the *words* that were spirit and life (John 6:63), and in my view constitute the flesh and blood. That would make sense if you realized that

He was the Word of God *and* the Bread of Life. The words are spirit because they are God's words and He is spirit. Eating His flesh and drinking His blood sounds like communion. I tried this, of course, as a practical application. That was not the concept. It was about speaking the words into one's life, the same theme we have already discussed. I memorized this passage and started speaking it every day. Guess what? God is faithful to this Word, and I am blessed with life through Him! It is very simple, but powerful and effective because of His grace.

So now, every day I speak this passage in John 6 into my life, I put on the Armor of God every day. What else? I have added the Lord's Prayer because it is so powerful and foundational, and one other passage; the one in 2Corinthians 10, "The weapons of our warfare are not of this world..." I memorized them all and speak those words over myself every day. I want the power of them in my life daily. There is tremendous transformative power and benefit to doing this on many levels.

Should you do what I do? That is between you and the Savior. I would recommend that you seek Him about it. There may be other passages that are better for you. I just want to expose you to the practice and you can decide if it would benefit you. It brings the Word of God to life in individual lives. It brings the power of truth to bear in the world we live in, not just in the stories of ancient times. It has been preserved for us by our God and Lord to transform us from worldly creatures to Spirit of God fueled sons of the Most High, living the Life; for Jesus is the Way, the Truth, and the Life (John 14:6), and His power is in those words.

I speak these words over myself sometime early in the day. If I am leaving the house, I usually recite them in the car. I know I am going to need it to face the funkiness (spiritual foulness) of the world I will be encountering.
It is very important to me to seek the Lord from the time I wake up. When I first wake up in the morning, I thank Him for His mercies.

> Through the LORD's mercies we are not consumed, because His compassions fail not. They are new every morning; great is Your faithfulness (Lamentations 3:22-23).

If I sense a positive sensation in my heart, I know there is mercy needed and I know it is one of three things: fear, doubt, or unbelief. Every issue seems to be rooted in one of these three things. I confess and repent of each until I feel a release of grace when the right one is addressed through repentance. Now, I can start the day with a "clean slate."

If I thank the Lord for His mercies, and sense a negative response, I know there is nothing from which to repent. This was a rarity to start with, but is becoming more frequent, by the Lord's grace.

I found another thing in the Word that the Lord does in the morning; He dispenses justice.

> The LORD within her is righteous; he does no wrong. Morning by morning he dispenses his justice, and every new day he does not fail, yet the unrighteous know no shame (Zephaniah 3:5).

Of course, I want to have His mercies first! Then I say, "Thank you Lord, that you dispense justice morning by morning." I am not sure what happens, but I do know it is powerful. I am sure it has to do with the realm of the spirit and those who try to operate in it against the truth. Then, I welcome the Holy Spirit and give Him authority over me that day (Romans 8:14). I clothe myself with Christ, by faith (Rather, clothe yourselves with the Lord Jesus Christ, and do not think about how to gratify the desires of the sinful nature [Romans 13:14]). Now, I am ready to quiet myself and listen for the "Word." Once I have received God's Word and have rejoiced in it, I am ready to get out of bed. I found the Lord waking me up before the alarm went off so that we could have this time together. It is amazingly powerful, encouraging, and precious. I never want to go without it again.

I realize that this may sound kind of formulaic and procedural. I am certainly not saying that one needs to do these things to be saved or loved by the Lord. They are, however, practical steps one can try to see if there is spiritual benefit to them for their own walk with God and encounter with Truth. This is a terrific way to draw near to the Lord because He is resident in the words of the Bible. They are who He is.

This is a different way of living. I would venture to guess that the world would not embrace all this as a lifestyle choice, like they do some other things, but it *is* reality. God's Word does stand forever, and the power of His Word is glory filled and unmistakable. My prayer is

Practical Christianity

that you have found something in this that you can use in your own walk with the Lord.

Chapter Twelve

Self Inflicted Wounds

For Christ did not send me to baptize, but to preach the gospel--not with words of human wisdom, lest the cross of Christ be emptied of its power (1Corinthians 1:17).

The last thing that any of us want to do is something that hinders the power of God from being manifest among us. In that power we have grace, love, peace, joy, wholeness, wellness, and freedom. We also have a precious closeness to the Lord that gives us a sense of who we really are and the blessings that we have coming on the horizon. This is the essence of hope, and hope gives us the wherewithal to go forward in peace, even when things are getting tumultuous around us.

Human nature is something that can be an issue when trying to keep the spiritual juices flowing. Some people feel like they should have the answers to the questions posed to them, and at times leaders in the church respond in human wisdom, having little else at their disposal. Their parishioners are looking for answers, and it would undermine the authority of the leadership if they could not respond adequately. We all have a need to be looked up to by our charges and our peers. Since we now have a basic understanding of the significance of our words, we realize that choosing words too quickly (James 1:9), or using our own understanding (Proverbs 3:5), can produce a less than desirable outcome. Scientific minds love to use logic, and logic is not a bad thing. I would like our political leaders to use it more. Logic, however, is based on premises (accepted assumptions), that, apart from God's Word, are rooted in human wisdom. Studying and embracing the Word of God changes our premises, and our logic is also different. This can put us at odds with "conventional" wisdom, and we must be prepared to deal with the consequences of this bit of misunderstanding. I believe it is called "carrying your cross."

There are other things that we do that will cause the virtual halt of the power of salvation to flow. One of the main ones is unforgiveness. This is a real killer, and something we should steer clear of with passion. When we forgive someone, we are not necessarily embracing or excusing their actions toward us. It does not mean that the relationship with them has to be restored. It is an internal act of giving the hurt and disappointment they caused us to the Lord. "Do not take revenge, my friends, but leave room for God's wrath, for it is written": It is mine to avenge; I will repay," says the Lord (Romans 12:19).

Forgiving others when they hurt us indicates to the Lord that while we did not appreciate what someone else may have done, we know that we are not perfect either, and we cannot place ourselves above others morally because of one circumstance. It also demonstrates trust that God sees what goes on and will take care of things in a way that takes a toll on *them*. Unforgiveness takes a toll on us. If I lash out at others in my pain and hurt, I am doubling the problem and becoming just as guilty as the other party. There are no winners there. Now, more people are getting punished, and the cycle never ends. There is no blessing in these circumstances. "Do not be overcome by evil, but overcome evil with good" (Romans 12:21).

Interestingly enough, the current rage in secular psychology is "forgiveness therapy." Even the unbelieving have seen the connection between harboring resentment and emotional ill health. I find that absolutely fascinating.

Our world is changing, friends, and principles of the Scripture are as widely accepted now as I have ever seen them in my lifetime. It is incredibly gratifying.

Another way to cutoff the heavenly flow is to rob God of what belongs to Him:

> "Will a man rob God? Yet you rob me. "But you ask, 'How do we rob you?' In tithes and offerings. You are under a curse--the whole nation of you--because you are robbing me (Malachi 3:8-9).

The only way you can rob someone is to take from them something that *belongs* to them. The Lord is indicating here, in my opinion, that those tithes and offering *do* belong to Him. If they are withheld, we are causing ourselves some harm. I realize that many people today think that churches and television preachers are only in what they do for the money. That may or may not be true, but it misses the point entirely. If it is His, He should decide what is done with it. This is another place where seeking the Lord for His will is very useful. Not every church is the same. If the church you are in seems too focused on something other than the Gospel of Christ or preaches the Word in a way that causes your spirit disquiet, you can go elsewhere. The point is that, like forgiveness, we do not do it for them; we do it for ourselves. It is an issue of obedience and submission. He says if we give, it will be given to us (Luke 6:38). We do it because the Lord wants that money to go into some form of ministry so that His Name will be glorified.

> Woe to you, teachers of the law and Pharisees, you hypocrites! You give a tenth of your spices--mint, dill and cumin. But you have neglected the more important matters of the law--justice, mercy and faithfulness. You should have practiced the latter, *without neglecting the former* (Matthew 23:23, emphasis mine).

Ministry takes on many forms. He may want the money to be used for your neighbor who needs groceries or needs a ride somewhere. He may want you to help out a co-worker, for His Name's sake. It is God's money, that He gave you the wherewithal to earn (Deuteronomy 8:18). We should ask Him where that money should go and how it would best honor Him. If the money is somehow misused, it does not undermine our obedience to God. He told us where He wanted it, and we honored His wishes. The consequences of that are between the Lord and whoever misused the money. If a man on the street uses the money for drugs, he is not squandering *your* money; he is squandering the Lord's money. The effect of those drugs will not be nearly the same, I can assure you. That disobedience *will* have a negative consequence. God is not mocked, "Do not be deceived: God cannot be mocked. A man reaps what he sows" (Galatians 6:7). Our concern is to make sure that we are sowing what is healthy and reaping God's fulfilled promises.

Fear is another killer of blessing, and it is a favored tool of evil in the war against truth.

> I tell you, my friends, do not be afraid of those who kill the body and after that can do no more. But I will show you whom you should fear: Fear him who, after the killing of the body, has power to throw you into hell. Yes, I tell you, fear him (Luke 12:4-5).

> But my righteous one will live by faith. And if he shrinks back, I will not be pleased with him. But we are not of those who shrink back and are destroyed, but of those who believe and are saved (Hebrews 10:38-39).

> But even if you should suffer for what is right, you are blessed. Do not fear what they fear; do not be frightened (1Peter 3:14).

> There is no fear in love. But perfect love
> drives out fear, because fear has to do with
> punishment. The one who fears is not made
> perfect in love (1John 4:18).

As was stated before, there is no doubt that the issues surrounding faith in Christ are extremely serious. It may help to keep in mind that it is not the death from this world to the next we should be most concerned about. It is what the Bible calls the "second death" that should have our full attention.

> But the cowardly, the unbelieving, the vile,
> the murderers, the sexually immoral, those
> who practice magic arts, the idolaters and all
> liars--their place will be in the fiery lake of
> burning sulfur. This is the second death
> (Revelation 21:8).

This is the motivating force behind my willingness to face whatever comes, trusting the Lord for His protection and grace. The first death is reasonably assured (except for Enoch, Elijah, Melchizedek, etc. or if we are "transformed in the twinkling of an eye" – 1Corinthians 15:52), the second death is something we should give our full effort to avoid.

As was stated in the Scripture in 1John 4 above, fear is an indication that love has not been perfected. This is something to focus on. Who does not want more love?

> For I am convinced that neither death nor life, neither angels nor demons, neither the present nor the future, nor any powers, neither height nor depth, nor anything else in all creation, will be able to separate us from the love of God that is in Christ Jesus our Lord (Romans 8:38).

It is challenging, but when you are going through a trial, please try to remember this passage and give thanks to the Lord for His love in spite of the circumstances you are facing. If you are suffering for His sake, you will feel His love and peace at that moment. It is so helpful and encouraging!

The thing about our relationship to the Lord that intrigues me is that He is working very hard to take us to a place where we can have the desire of our hearts (Psalms 37:4). The ones fighting and resisting Him the most are us, because we are having a hard time trusting that He is in charge and He knows what He is doing. In what we endure, we wonder if there is a positive purpose behind it and if God is using it for our good and His glory: He does. Our fears are what keep us from resting in Him and trusting Him. We end up running away from our blessings and His grace. Doing the opposite will ensure that your prayers are heard and that answers are forthcoming.

Chapter Thirteen

The Fruit of the Spirit

By their fruit you will recognize them. Do people pick grapes from thornbushes, or figs from thistles? (Matthew 7:16)

The beauty of our Savior is that He knows us personally and He knows our heart. We do not need to try and act like we are doing something just to impress Him. Likewise, we may seem to be struggling outwardly, but He knows what is going on inside of us.

I remember my Mom, an unbeliever, asking me how I could call myself a Christian when I still smoked and drank. I was a young believer then and knew I was struggling. I had cried out to the Lord about my issues and was trusting Him and waiting on Him for help. One thing I told the Lord when I got saved was that I could not pretend to be something I was not. I knew that the Lord would work things out, but at that time I was hopelessly addicted to nicotine.

I told my Mom that Christianity was something I believed in. I trusted Jesus as my Lord and was seeking

Him for help with my issues. I was comforted to know that the Lord loved me in spite of my issues, and that it was not what a man took into his body that made him unclean. "But by faith we eagerly await through the Spirit the righteousness for which we hope" (Galatians 5:5). She accepted what I told her graciously and years later came to know the Lord prior to her passing. Praise God!

I was in the process of becoming Spirit-minded. "The mind of sinful man is death, but the mind controlled by the Spirit is life and peace..." (Romans 8:6). So, like we discussed earlier, taking the Word into our hearts by reading it, hearing it preached, or speaking it over ourselves, has an impact in our hearts. "Consequently, faith comes from hearing the message, and the message is heard through the word of Christ" (Romans 10:17). The Word resides in our heart (Psalms 119:11). The heart is the source of our thoughts. "For as he thinks in his heart, so is he" (Proverbs 23:7a, NKJV). From the heart, our words are also originated: "For out of the overflow of the heart the mouth speaks (Matthew 12:34b). Our words convey power, and if we can harness our tongues, speaking words of truth and life, we grow and become better able to keep ourselves and our desires in check (James 3:2): "So I say, live by the Spirit, and you will not gratify the desires of the sinful nature" (Galatians 5: 16).

Living by the Spirit produces the fruit of the Spirit: "But the fruit of the Spirit is love, joy, peace, patience, kindness, goodness, faithfulness, gentleness, and self-control" (Galatians 5:22).

Self control; this is another counterintuitive term. Scripture is full of interesting paradoxes: we must die to find life, give in order to receive, submit to God in order to be free, and now be filled with the Spirit to have *self* control.

It really is true, though, and well worth the effort. I have not smoked or drank in many years (I am not keeping track of the dates). God was faithful and delivered me in my seeking Him and desire to be free.

Bearing the fruit of the Spirit is a crucial aspect of successful Christian living. It is so noticeable that people are drawn to it and God is glorified by its existence. It is an outward indication of our internal situation or as I like to say, "a physical manifestation of our spiritual condition."

"You did not choose me, but I chose you and appointed you to go and bear fruit--fruit that will last. Then the Father will give you whatever you ask in my name" (John 15:16). Do you hear the promise and condition in this passage? It is saying that if we bear the fruit, *then* the Father will give you whatever you ask. This should underscore the eternal value and evangelistic magnetism that bearing good fruit represents. Ever heard someone ask, "Why are you so happy all the time?" or, "How come you can handle things so well? You never seem to lose your cool." Is this an opportunity to give God glory? I should say so!

Maintaining a fruitful Christian life is very challenging, but very worthwhile. Some of the principles we have discussed in this book will help in that endeavor. The dark side of our world will oppose the bearing of that fruit, but the Word of God is powerful to save. Imagine what good fruit will do in marriages, homes, and children - not to mention churches, communities, and nations.

May the God who watches over His Word to perform it bless you as you rest in His grace and walk in His love!